Grieving, Sharing, Healing

A Guide for Facilitating Early Adolescent Bereavement Groups

Rekha Murthy
Lisa-Loraine Smith

Research Press
2612 North Mattis Avenue
Champaign, Illinois 61822
[800] 519-2707
www.researchpress.com

The authors gratefully acknowledge Interfaith Neighbors, Inc.,
for its guidance in producing the following illustrations: Window to My Soul,
Looking Backward . . . Looking Forward, and Feelings Sheet.

The authors gratefully acknowledge permission from Prof. Roselle Kurland of Hunter
College School of Social Work for the following descriptions: (a) group development during the
beginning stage, page 96; (b) group development during the middle stage, page 124; and
(c) group development during the ending stage, page 147. We also acknowledge her permission
for providing her development of a model for pre-group planning, consisting of seven
components, on page 34.

Copies of this book may be ordered from Research Press
at the address given on the title page.

Composition by Jeff Helgesen
Cover design by Linda Brown, Positive I.D. Graphic Design, Inc.
Printed by Bang Printing

ISBN 0–87822–501–3
Library of Congress Control Number 2004096614

*To the memory of our loved ones, who in death
continue to inspire us and infuse us with strength:
Rekha's father and brother, D. V. K. Murthy and Ravindra "Rev" Murthy
Lisa's grandparents, Loraine and Louis Drucker and Esther and Ben Smith
Our dear friend and colleague Brenda L. Robinson*

Contents

Acknowledgments

Without the help of so many resilient adolescents and the aid and support of countless and concerned professionals and agencies, the Children's Bereavement Project (CBP) could not have become such a resounding success.

We are indebted to our colleagues at Interfaith Neighbors, Inc., and within the CBP for their continued support over the years. Our most heartfelt thanks go to our mentor and former executive director, Eileen Lyons, who always believed in the strength of this program. She embraced it fully, advised us on all of our ideas, and worked unceasingly first to create and then to expand the CBP into the hub of strength it has become.

We are grateful to the many individuals and foundations that have provided financial support over the years. In particular, for providing us with a generous grant that helped to launch our program, we owe our thanks to the Open Society Institute of the Soros Foundation—Project on Death in America. Other foundations, agencies, and programs that have supported us include the van Ameringen Foundation, the Heckscher Foundation, the Charles A. Frueauff Foundation, the Eastman Foundation, the NYC Board of Education, All Souls Church, Brick Church, Heavenly Rest Church, St. James Church, Blue Hill Troupe, Ltd., In Lieu of Flowers, and the Interfaith Neighbors, Inc., Board of Directors.

This book and curriculum could not have been written without the support and feedback of so many. The following individuals (listed in alphabetical order) provided important observations and suggestions for the book: Mahesh Ananth, Ida Benton, Nancy Bermack, Roberta Bernstein, Clayton Evans, Jocelyn Forman, Jerry Gips, Sharon Gold, Rick Greenberg, Kate Greenfield, Dianne Kangisser, Chris Kido, Rosemary LeBron, Eileen Lyons, Andrew Malekoff, Cheryl Mwaria, Barbara Ruth Jena Drucker Smith, Ed Sunderland, Maritza Villegas, Alice Vogt, Phyllis Wender, Paul Whyte, Kimberly Sproule Wright, and Randye Jana Zerman.

We owe a special debt of gratitude to two key people—the late Ravindra "Rev" Murthy for his endless support and the keen editorial observations he provided during countless nights of reviewing this manuscript, and Paul Handman, who pored over voluminous research on adolescent bereavement and graciously provided his editing skills on early drafts of our work.

We would also like to acknowledge sincerely our publishing company, Research Press, Inc., and its president, Ann Wendel, for giving us a means through which to spread this important work. Moreover, we owe much thanks to David Hamburg, whose editorial skills and dedication brought to fruition a smooth and polished product, and to Jeff Helgesen, production manager, for his overall organization and design of this text.

The CBP could not exist without the relationships we developed with the middle schools of Districts 4 and 2 in Manhattan. These include the Academy of Environmental Science, the Academy of Health and Sciences, East Harlem Career Academy, East Harlem Performing Arts School, Harbor Performing Arts Academy, Hurston Academy, Isaac Newton School for Science and Math, Manhattan East, Manhattan West, Maritime Academy, New York Prep, Rafael Cordero Bilingual Academy, Robert Wagner Junior High School, School for the Physical City, and Talented and Gifted Institute for Young Scholars. Of course, our program itself would not exist without the inspiration provided by the adolescents we have worked with since our inception in 1994. We thank them for sharing their lives with us.

Finally, we would like to thank our families for reminding us to follow our dreams—our parents: Radha Murthy and the late D. V. Krishna Murthy and Barbara Ruth Jena Drucker Smith and Richard Ellis Smith; our brothers: the late Ravindra "Rev" Murthy and Eric Drucker Smith; our husbands: Mahesh Ananth and Jerry Gips; and our children: Kathan Murthy Ananth and Anya Esther Smith Gips.

Foreword

Grief amplifies and complicates the typical strains of early adolescence—a stage of development that sparks a realignment of emotional attachments, a cluster of physical and cognitive changes, and a bevy of behaviors that test the waters of adulthood and mimic the pleasures and pains of childhood. To adolescents, the death of a loved one yields a cruel irony: The adolescent's tentative efforts to be independent, separate, and grown up are suddenly and unexpectedly experienced in abrupt, unforgiving terms. Angry words of rebellion, such as "I wish you were dead" or "I can't wait to get away from you," can haunt the adolescent, whose safe parameters for experimentations with independence are shattered by the death of a parent.

It is in the context of this precarious stage of human development from which the grief of a 10- to 15-year-old can best be understood; clues to the adolescent's suffering can be unearthed, as can methods to help and support the adolescent. *Grieving, Sharing, and Healing* offers a keen look at the struggle of the early adolescent who, amid this swirl of change, comes to terms with death, loss, and grief. By working with groups of adolescents—all of whom are in grief—the authors have helped adolescents to help each other to cope. This practice of mutual aid, with an age group that is particularly vulnerable, is the focus of *Grieving, Sharing, and Healing*. It is a book that captures both the singular learning backgrounds and the multifarious experiences of authors Rekha Murthy and Lisa-Loraine Smith, two social workers—teammates at a New York City community-based organization—who set out to help inner-city adolescents who had experienced the loss of a loved one. They worked with hundreds of inner-city adolescents, conducting bereavement groups in their middle and junior high schools during the school day; the reach of their efforts grew, and eventually became the Children's Bereavement Project (CBP), an invaluable offshoot of Interfaith Neighbors, Inc.

Grieving, Sharing, and Healing is written for the group facilitator who is either thinking about, planning to engage in, or currently working with adolescents in grief. Because it is a tool that guides reflection and inquiry, this book can be useful at any stage of the facilitator's efforts to address the needs of this specific population. Its curriculum is neither a silver bullet nor an airtight formula, but rather a body of work that captures the themes and elements of bereavement work with adolescents. It remains in the hands of the reader to discern the contextual issues that will shape his or her use of its tools and activities. The population, the setting, the time limitations, the facilitator's own skills, and a range of other factors will need to be taken into account in the planning, implementation, and evaluation of a new bereavement group.

The core elements that this guide offers are shaped by the unique parameters within which the authors have conducted their practices. Effective group leadership is part art, part science, and by definition, adaptive. While guiding groups through their stages of development, facilitators will draw on science (i.e., their knowledge of the process of grief, adolescent development, and social group work as well as their ability to employ a complex set of practice skills). The "art" of the work lies in the personal characteristics and unique styles of the group facilitators. Their ability to build strong connections between and among group members is enhanced by their warmth, empathy, optimism, and proper use of self.

The relationships that facilitators build with group members, including how and what they share of their own losses, is of central importance to working with adolescents in grief. The authors maintain that by sharing information about their own losses and by modeling the curriculum activities, they are helping group members to normalize the process of grief. This purposeful use of self, or "personal sharing," has its detractors. For example, some colleagues feel that facilitators' discussion of their own losses represents a type of violation, an overstepping of sacred bounds between group members and their facilitators. Other critics suggest that promoting mutual aid between and among group members will undermine the facilitator's role; still others worry that it will preempt group members' feelings by focusing the spotlight on the facilitator, thereby tampering with transference.

We strongly recommend that facilitators carefully consider any decision to share personal information with group members. It was our experience, however, that the expertise and sensitivity of two highly proficient social workers with post–masters-level training came into play, as their divulging of information about a personal loss proved beneficial to individual group members and to the group as a whole. In focus groups and on questionnaires, members repeatedly cited the facilitator's disclosure as a "bridge" moment—one that helped group members to feel less isolated, more accepted, and more willing to share personal information: Many members described the group facilitator's discussion of her loss as a special gift that helped to build a bridge of compassion and understanding. Perhaps, among inner-city adolescents who regularly feel the sting of bias and "being seen as different," this intervention serves to break down perceived barriers. As we straddle the border between art and science, it is vital that the facilitator responsibly handle this suggested use of self.

Grieving, Sharing, and Healing emphasizes the facilitator's central responsibility to build a culture of mutual aid within the bereavement group—a place where members *help each other* to cope. Repeatedly, our experiences showed that group members experienced an *epiphany,* an "aha" moment, when they realized that they were not alone, that their peers in grief experienced thoughts and feelings much like their own. Helping group members to reach this insight, so deeply rooted in the need of the early adolescent to feel *normal,* constitutes a core element of working with early adolescents in grief. It also represents the authors' fundamental belief in mutual aid as a healing tool, and their unwillingness to *pathologize* grief.

The CBP, which got under way in 1994, changed the lives of the staff involved and transformed the culture of Interfaith Neighbors, Inc., the social service organization that gave birth to it. Like so many Interfaith initiatives, the bereavement program had a humble beginning. It was born at a large, rectangular wooden table situated in the center's hub. That table was the setting for a medley of activities: During the morning and early afternoon, it was home to staff meetings, training exercises, and exciting brainstorming sessions; after 3:00 p.m., when adolescents streamed in at the end of their school day, the wooden table became the focal point of tutoring sessions, rap groups, and an assortment of art projects and board games. One day, in the midst of that hum of kinship, it dawned on us that the adolescents with whom we worked were experiencing death, grief, and loss, and that we hadn't responded to their needs other than on an *ad hoc* basis—almost as an anomaly that we dealt with as an afterthought. Without fanfare, without committed funding, and without a clue as to what we would discover, the Interfaith Neighbors staff began to contemplate the following question: In what ways do grief and loss affect the lives of the adolescents and families with whom we work? The cerebral and visceral journey that followed was both ordinary and extraordinary, embracing a uniquely human and humane continuum of professional and personal experiences.

Stepping forward, then, in an act that was designed to gain a better understanding of the lives of the people with whom we work, was the perfect step. And so, supported by that solid foundation, we moved forward and assumed a stance of inquiry. We discovered that about 75 percent of the adolescents who participated in our agency programs had lost a loved one. We also found that, in poor inner-city and primarily minority neighborhoods, our adolescents experienced loss routinely. Our staff conducted outreach in East Harlem schools, where we asked students to indicate, by a show of hands, if they had experienced the death of a loved one. In some classes, every hand shot up. We researched the statistics and learned that more than 1.2 million adolescents (about 4 percent nationwide) will lose a parent by the age of 15. The Columbine shooting, and later, the tragedy of Sept. 11, 2001, renewed our focus on the issue of grief, long an epidemic among inner-city adolescents. Few programs, we would discover, concentrate on the bereavement needs of adolescents, whether inner-city adolescents or not; even fewer programs are built to help facilitators to work with *groups* of adolescents. *Grieving, Sharing, and Healing* is a direct response to countless requests for directions on how to work with youth in grief.

The CBP had a major impact on its parent organization, Interfaith Neighbors, Inc. We began to acknowledge both explicitly and implicitly the role of grief in so many adolescents' lives and, as a result, changed the methods we employed as well as the culture of the agency itself. We started to ask adolescents, during initial psychosocial interviews, about losses in their lives. We asked parents. We became more comfortable with the language of loss and grief so that barriers to talking about grief began to topple. At the center of the agency, the heart of the general program room—and just a few feet from our worn wooden table—we asked the adolescents to erect a memorial wall. Ceramic tiles, each hand-painted by an adolescent, were used to memorialize their loved ones. As we stood before the wall, it became clear that adolescents had lost parents, grandparents, aunts, uncles, and siblings. This memorial wall—resplendent in bright, proud colors—stood as a testament to the agency's new norms, which embraced and accepted death as a part of all our lives.

Perhaps, as we look back, it is not so strange that the agency had grown in such a way that it became a respite for staff. During the past decade, several staff members have experienced tragic personal losses, prompting all of us to marvel at how fortunate it is for them and for us that they work at Interfaith Neighbors, a place where people in grief feel deeply understood and accepted. The sense of comfort felt by these staff members, like that felt by our adolescent group members, was derived from the realization that they were not alone, that the universality of loss and grief links all of us together in a precious bond of need and compassion.

—-Eileen Lyons
Former Executive Director
Interfaith Neighbors, Inc.

Preface

The Children's Bereavement Project (CBP) is a program that is an offshoot of Interfaith Neighbors, Inc., a community-based organization in New York City that provides educational and social work services to adolescents, teachers, clinicians, and group facilitators. The mission of Interfaith Neighbors is to enable adolescents to discover their strengths; flourish as individuals; and become responsible, caring community members. Invigorating and rejuvenating the vulnerable adolescent—the adolescent who has experienced trauma, death, or chronic academic failure—constitute our special interest and our distinctive competence.

The CBP was founded in 1994, when we began asking adolescents during classroom outreach if they had experienced the death of a loved one. The response was overwhelming—more than 75 percent of our adolescents raised their hands. We began running school-based bereavement support groups in a few schools in the East Harlem and Yorkville areas of Manhattan. The groups started out informally, almost like rap groups, but the closeness and healing process they engendered made clear the groups' mission.

Further conversations with teachers and guidance counselors strengthened our resolve by making us realize that early and violent death is pervasive in the lives and families of untold numbers of adolescents. With school personnel and parents reporting that they felt ill equipped to assist their young grievers, the demand to expand this program grew, and the need to keep it blossoming became paramount. Together with our first executive director, Eileen Lyons, we worked to create the multidisciplinary curriculum that we have developed and honed. News of this burgeoning program spread, and with eager, widespread support, we branched out from a program that was offered at only a few schools to one that was available at more than 15 different schools in East Harlem. More than 1,200 adolescents, all bonded through death, have participated in the CBP, and the past few years have been a journey of strength, struggles, and inspiration.

Our decision to provide extensive group services was predicated on our belief that mutual aid groups offer a variety of healing factors, and that the peer group setting is vitally important to meeting the needs of adolescents. Our 12-week bereavement group curriculum provides suggested activities and discussion topics to be used in accordance with the beginning, middle, and ending stages of each group. Various modalities, such as writing, art, discussion, and reading, are used to effect communication between and among group members and facilitators as well as to foster group cohesion.

Unfortunately, adolescents learn early in life that polite society actively avoids mention of death, media actively glorify death, and adults often feel that adolescents are "too young" to understand death. Adolescents receive both direct and indirect messages to "get over" a death rather than to "work through" a death. Burdened with subtle pressure to grieve quickly, many adolescents feel different from their peers, or perhaps they feel reluctant to talk about their emotions. Therefore, it is vital that they have a safe place to talk about death and safe, caring people with whom to talk about their feelings. Bereavement groups provide them with this unique opportunity.

We have seen over time that the group experience enables adolescents to talk about death because it does in fact provide a safe environment. Adolescents who have rarely discussed their losses are at last finding their voices and realizing—many for the first time—that they are not alone in their struggles. The safety of the group allows adolescents to express emotions and to know that it's OK to confront feelings that they used to be unable to talk about, such as regret, anger, and guilt. At long last, they are telling their stories and being heard.

Since news of the success of the CBP has spread, we have received countless requests for training regimens and activities to use with youth in grief. Those of us who work with youth are accustomed to encountering adolescents who are affected by death and are struggling to make sense of something that's difficult to comprehend for adults as well as adolescents. We earnestly hope that this book be considered by bereavement group facilitators as a useful, effective tool in their work with adolescents. Although much of the information in the book focuses on the school environment, the curriculum is intended for use in a variety of settings where adolescents are found, including clinics, religious institutions, hospitals, and community centers.

This two-part book examines many important issues pertaining to grieving adolescents. Part I consists of six chapters: Chapter 1 addresses the needs of adolescents in grief; chapter 2 explores the beneficial aspects of mutual aid bereavement groups; chapter 3 discusses how to form and run a bereavement group; chapter 4 examines the responsibilities and characteristics of facilitators in mutual aid bereavement groups; chapter 5 describes the three stages of bereavement groups; and chapter 6 discusses bereavement groups in schools. Part II consists of chapters 7, 8, and 9, which provide activities that are earmarked for each of the three stages discussed in chapter 5 and examine more closely the specifics of our 12-week curriculum. The book ends with an afterword that briefly evaluates the group experience and discusses the value of follow-up.

Grief is a lifelong process—and a personal one as well. We hope that the tools developed by the CBP will help break the taboo of acknowledging and discussing death and its effects on adolescent survivors. We also hope that this curriculum continues to empower adolescents who are grieving—to strengthen their voices and open wide the door to the healing process once and for all.

PART

I

CHAPTER

1

Adolescents in Grief

When we at the Children's Bereavement Project (CBP) visit junior high and middle school classrooms in New York City to discuss our bereavement groups, we ask all the adolescents to raise their hands if they have experienced the death of a loved one during the course of their lives. Almost always, a clear majority of them do indeed raise their hands. What this tells us, among other things, is that grief is not an experience reserved only for adults, but rather one that affects adolescents as well.

Although supportive services, such as individual and family counseling, can offer adolescents the opportunity to receive support for this difficult, life-changing event, they need more help than they are getting. It is hoped that more help will give them the chance to fare better in the long run: emotionally, socially, and academically. But before we can help, we need to know the answers to some questions. For example, who are these adolescents who have suffered loss at such a young age, and what risks do they face as a result of their having lost a loved one at such a young age? In this chapter, we outline different facets of the problem of adolescents in grief: who they are, what they feel, and what affects their grieving and healing process.

IMPORTANT COMPONENTS OF ADOLESCENT GRIEF

The terms *grief* and *mourning* and *bereaved* are defined differently. On the basis of our experience, we define grief as one's personal reactions and coping mechanisms to a death—one's feelings, thoughts, actions, and physical responses (Baxter & Stuart, 1999). What we show of our grief reaction in public is often referred to as mourning, which encompasses a broad range of societal, cultural, and religious rituals for addressing death and its aftermath. We use the term bereaved to refer to one who has experienced a personal death, such as the death of a close family member, a friend, or a loved one.

Adolescents are not immune to the grieving process. In fact, the death of a parent or other significant person during one's adolescence

3

carries consequences that may last a lifetime. Following a death, adolescents will most often find that their daily life changes in a number of ways; their role in their family will be affected, and so will their relationships with their friends and other peers. They may even experience academic difficulty and behavior problems that place them at an increased risk of dropping out of school. In essence, grieving will fundamentally affect their transition to adulthood.

During our bereavement group sessions, we have participated in countless conversations about death. Adolescents often say they receive both direct and indirect messages about how they should grieve and for how long. These messages may come from their own families, the media, the community, or even themselves. Beginning with our initial interaction with an adolescent, we feel it is imperative to emphasize and reemphasize the following realities about grief:

Grief is a normal and important reaction to a death. All people grieve, but in their own way. Some people feel comfortable crying in public, whereas others feel decidedly uncomfortable. Some find that participating in sports and other activities provides a more satisfactory outlet through which to express their grief, whereas others believe that doing so is disrespectful. Regardless of how one grieves, it is important to keep in mind that just because people may not look sad on the outside does not mean they are not grieving on the inside.

When we are grieving, our moods and feelings may change often and suddenly. Certain thoughts, sights, sounds, and smells may trigger a grief response at any moment. Simply put, the death of someone close is a life-altering event, and the grief that we experience can remain with us for as long as we live. Although the passage of time may afford some healing, grief is a lifelong process that is bound to feel more intense at certain times than at others. Special days, such as birthdays or anniversaries, are likely to trigger feelings of grief every year. The length of time that one experiences particular grief reactions depends on the individual. Contrary to the concept of "stages of grief," adolescents have told us that they experience a range of feelings, but not necessarily in any particular order or for any particular amount of time. Because of this, we encourage adolescents and those who work with them not to think about grief in terms of consecutive and distinct stages.

Grief affects many aspects of our life, including our home life, our school life, our interactions with friends, the way we feel about ourselves, and what we think about the world. Consequently, there is no one right way or wrong way to grieve. Rather, grieving is a process that is unique to each individual and influenced by many factors, including, but not limited to, the relationship we had with the person who died, the amount of support we receive from others, the manner in which the person died, our personality and experience with death, and our cultural and religious beliefs.

Some adolescents find certain activities and experiences helpful as they attempt to adjust to life without the person who died. These pursuits include being with and talking to other adolescents who are grieving, as would be the case in a bereavement group; writing stories or poems or drawing pictures that depict their feelings; talking about and remembering the person who died; and creating ways to incorporate the deceased into their lives, perhaps through rituals and ceremonies.

Some adolescents who are grieving may become involved in self-destructive behavior in an effort to avoid the pain of the loss. They may, for example, engage in risky sexual behavior or use alcohol or drugs. They may also become either aggressive or withdrawn.

WHY ADOLESCENTS TURN TO BEREAVEMENT GROUPS

During the first day of the bereavement group, we ask group members what motivated them to join the group. Often, one or more adolescents will respond, "I wanted to be in this group because I want to share my feelings, and I want to know how other people feel." Usually, they add, they feel uncomfortable discussing their feelings about the death with those around them; however, they are eager to do so in a group composed of peers who have experienced a similar kind of loss.

Because of the group's reservations about discussing their feelings about the death—and in an effort to help them feel more comfortable—we begin our curriculum in Part II with an activity called the Feelings Sheet (see **Week 1**, on **page 99** of **chapter 7**). In this activity, group members are asked to identify some of their feelings about joining the group and about the death of their loved one. This activity helps them to determine the types of feelings they have in common as well as those that are unique to particular members. (It should be kept in mind that, although death in this book will be referred to in the singular, some adolescents will be working through the loss of more than one friend or loved one.)

Throughout the group, members will continue to identify and share their feelings with one another. On the next-to-last day of the group, members are asked to repeat the Feelings Sheet activity to see whether they can gauge any changes in their feelings since the beginning of the group.

From our years of experience working and learning from adolescents in grief, we have discovered that there exist almost an infinite number of feelings about death. Some feelings are more universal, whereas others are less so. All feelings, however, are important to acknowledge, identify, and discuss with adolescents within the group. Helping adolescents to express their feelings is a crucial element of the grieving process.

Within the group context, adolescents often realize that others share their feelings, and this discovery serves to normalize their emotions; consequently, they begin to feel more normal rather than more abnormal, or alienated. Following are some thoughts on a range of feelings that adolescents may have after a loss.

Anger: Many adolescents report feeling angry after the death of a loved one. It is perfectly normal to feel this emotion as one struggles to adjust after a death. Adolescents may feel angry about the death in general, certain that life has dealt them a bad hand, or they may direct their anger at any number of individuals for either playing or not playing specific roles in the death. This anger may be directed at the perpetrator (if a crime was involved), the victim, surviving family members, friends, the doctors, or the police. Depending on their religious beliefs, adolescents may also feel angry at God.

Anxiety: Feelings of anxiety are very common after a death. Adolescents may be afraid that something bad may happen to them or to others they care about. They may feel less secure in their surroundings and sense that life in general is more fragile. Some adolescents may have actual anxiety attacks, which are often characterized by palpitations, sweating, trembling, shortness of breath, abdominal pain or nausea, dizziness, and a strong feeling of immobilization (DSM-IV, 1994). If anxiety attacks do occur, it is important for the adolescent's parent or guardian to consult a mental health professional to schedule a thorough evaluation. Some adolescents also feel jittery about joining a bereavement group. Although talking in front of a group and sharing personal information provokes anxiety in many adolescents, we have found that this anxiety usually subsides in time.

Apathy: We have found that some adolescents appear indifferent after a death. This reaction may serve as a coping mechanism intended to shield adolescents from the harshness and shock of their new, unexpected situation. Indifference may protect them from further disappointment and pain. Adolescents sometimes report feeling so down that they simply do not care about much in their life anymore. This is one of several situations in which further evaluation for depression and potential suicide is warranted.

Caution: Oftentimes, a death can shatter one's trust in how one believes the world is supposed to work. Many of the adolescents in our bereavement groups have said that after experiencing a death, they feel more cautious about trusting people and afraid to invest their love and friendship in people for fear that these people, too, may die or leave them.

Confusion: Death is often a confusing phenomenon because it generates many unanswered questions about life. Adolescents may feel confused about why things happened the way they did and why these things happened to them.

Fear: Following the death of a loved one, many adolescents report experiencing new fears. For example, they may fear being left alone, fear their own mortality, or fear being harmed. They may have nightmares about the way their loved one died, or they may encounter scary visions of their loved ones—visions that leave them shaken.

Guilt: Many adolescents feel guilty when a loved one dies. They may feel as though they did not do enough to help the loved one in a time of need or in time to prevent the death. They may feel bad about the way they treated the loved one in the past and may even blame themselves for the death if, for example, in a fit of anger they once felt or stated that they wished the person would die. For those adolescents who have lost a loved one to suicide, feelings of guilt may be especially pronounced. These adolescents may blame themselves for missing important signs of the loved one's impending suicide and not doing enough to prevent the suicide.

Jealousy: As adolescents attempt to adjust after a death, they may feel jealous that their peers are not facing the same struggle. They may feel that their entire personal world has been altered, while, at the same time, the outside world has stayed the same. Adolescents often report feeling pangs of jealousy as they watch mothers with their sons or see grandfathers with their grandchildren. They feel jealous that they themselves will never again be able to experience these feelings that they once felt.

Loneliness: Adolescents often say they feel "different" after a death occurs. They feel that their experience of loss has isolated them from their peers, many of whom may not have encountered a similar experience and are thus truly unable to understand what these grieving adolescents are going through. This leaves the grieving adolescents feeling empty, alone, and isolated. Many adolescents also feel lonely simply because they miss their loved ones and the emotions that accompanied those relationships.

Regret: Quite often, adolescents wish they could have changed some aspect of their relationship with the deceased. Some may wish that they could have spent more time with the loved one or had the opportunity to say and do certain things. Regret may be especially pronounced in situations where a loved one died suddenly.

Relief: Some adolescents feel relief after a loved one dies. For example, if the deceased suffered from a chronic or terminal illness and was in considerable and constant pain, the adolescent may feel relief because the loved one is no longer suffering. In situations in which adolescents endured a conflicted or abusive relationship with the person who died, or if the deceased participated in risky or unhealthy behavior, these adolescents may feel relief not to be involved in or subjected to those circumstances.

Sadness: This is perhaps the emotion that is most commonly expressed by adolescents. Most adolescents express a general feeling of being sad, of struggling to enjoy things going on around them, of having a heavy heart and feeling empty. Sadness is one of the emotions that adolescents expect they are supposed to feel after the death of a loved one.

Shock: Feelings of shock and denial are very common after a death. The reality and finality of death takes time to sink in, and adolescents often report feeling in shock as they attempt to sort through the many changes in their lives that death brings.

HOW GRIEVING AFFECTS THE DEVELOPMENT OF ADOLESCENTS

In the CBP, we do comprehensive intakes, or assessments, with each potential group member, which allow us to learn more about the grief experience and loss history of that particular adolescent. Grieving is unique to each adolescent. A number of distinct variables affect the nature, substance, and timing of the healing process (Kandt, 1994; Grollman, 1977; Hodges, 1988). When working with adolescents in grief, it is important that group facilitators keep all of the following variables in mind because they will help to provide a more comprehensive picture of an adolescent's specific situation and special needs.

Growing Up

No longer children, and not quite adults either, adolescents face many new challenges and responsibilities, some exciting and some scary. At this time in their lives, adolescents really begin to get to know themselves—their interests, values, morals, and goals. They experience pronounced physical changes and heightened libido. They begin to develop their own autonomy and separate more from parents and guardians as they begin to gravitate more toward their friends for support and advice. They also begin to develop more abstract methods of thinking and reasoning.

Adolescence, with all of its inherent changes, is challenging enough without the interference of additional trauma or loss. The developmental changes in adolescents are complicated greatly by the death of a loved one and the grieving process that accompanies it. Adults commonly misjudge the depth of grief that an adolescent is capable of experiencing. Adolescents are left to ponder the state of the relationships in their lives, not only with the person who died but with others as well. The particulars of the death may also torment them, as adolescents attempt to grapple with the manner in which a loved one died, possible unresolved issues or regrets, changing life roles and responsibilities, and difficulty identifying and expressing their feelings (The Dougy Center, 1999).

Although the precise impact of a death on an adolescent's development is unique to each adolescent, during our conversations with them, we have observed some common reactions and thoughts and feelings. Here are a few things the adolescents in our groups have taught us about how their grieving experiences affect their development:

▷ At a time when they want to be free to have fun with their friends, they feel burdened by the heaviness of their grief. They feel "different" from their peers because of their death experience and often isolate themselves from friends and social gatherings.

▷ They feel conflicted about spending time with their family and surviving parent or guardian, if in fact there is a surviving adult. They may worry about their family and, as a result, feel awkward as they become more dependent and attached to parents or other adults in their life at the same time that their peers are separating from their parents and becoming more independent. Some adolescents feel weighed down by what they perceive as an obligation to take care of and spend time with their family, when they would rather occupy their time with their friends and not have to think about the death and the sadness that accompanies it.

▷ Some adolescents report feeling extremely self-conscious about the physical changes they are experiencing, almost as if the death has left them feeling naked. Others find that their grief serves to lessen the preoccupation with physical changes that many of their peers are experiencing.

▷ After a death—and often in an attempt to suppress some of their loneliness—adolescents try to invest the bulk of their emotional energy in intimate relationships with boyfriends or girlfriends. They may use sexual activity as a means to "forget" their grief and, as a consequence, find themselves in vulnerable and potentially dangerous situations.

▷ Many adolescents find that their perception of how the world is supposed to work is greatly affected by the death of a close friend or loved one. They may find themselves in a sort of existential crisis—pondering the meaning of life and the unfairness of death, struggling to define their morals and values and reasons for being. Working in the inner city, we have found that repeated exposure to death and violence often leads adolescents to question their own mortality and makes them fearful of dying young. For some of them, their bubble of invincibility may burst; for others, a desire may take hold to display an indifference to life and take part in risky behaviors merely to test the limits of safety.

▷ Adolescents' newly developed abstract thinking allows them to have an adult understanding and concept of death. They are able to understand the universality and finality of death. However, many of them struggle with figuring out their own religious and spiritual beliefs and integrating them into their grieving process.

Relationship with the Deceased

The various ways in which adolescents grieve naturally are affected by the relationships they had with the deceased and the roles they played in their lives. After all, when someone dies, we do not lose just that one person; we lose the relationship we had with that person (Wolfelt, 1996). The quality of the relationship, the interactions we had with that person—those are what we miss.

Understandably, we are sometimes quick to assume that certain losses are more severe or more important than others. Yet adolescents who lose the grandparents who reared them may, to some people's surprise, experience grief reactions quite similar to adolescents who lose the parents or guardians who reared them. The true nature of the relationships affects the grieving process because that is what disappears whenever someone dies: A daughter may no longer be "Daddy's little girl"; a boy may have lost the cousin who always defended or protected him. And, sadly, for those who for some reason were unable to form the kinds of relationships with the deceased that they may have hoped for, there is the loss of what never was and what never will be.

In our bereavement groups, we value and place tremendous emphasis on helping adolescents to identify what their loved ones represented to them and to incorporate the strengths, weaknesses, triumphs, and struggles of those relationships into our discussions and activities. We recognize the surety that, for every adolescent, the death of a parent, guardian, sibling, friend, grandparent, or caregiver will affect the grief process in ways that are unique to that adolescent. The group forum is an ideal place for them to engage in the grieving process because it allows them to reflect on who died, how their life has changed as a result, and what the deceased represented and still represents to them in so many different ways.

Contrary to grief theory that suggests that successful grieving requires survivors to separate from or "say goodbye" to the deceased loved one, we advocate a style of grief expression that enables and encourages adolescents to develop methods of maintaining connections to their loved ones after the death has occurred (Vickio, 1999; Attig, 1996). As we will show later in this book, our curriculum contains activ-

ities that allow adolescents to accomplish this goal—t
staying in touch with their deceased loved ones.

Cause of Death

How a person dies is also a vital factor in the healing process of one who
grieves. When adolescents lose a loved one to an abrupt and unexpected death (e.g., homicide, suicide, accident, acute illness), it is often
the case that they did not have a chance to communicate certain
thoughts and sentiments to the person before the death, to be able to
talk things out with the deceased and address any unresolved issues or
regrets. Consequently, their perception of safety and control is challenged
because they must now try to deal with feelings of vulnerability caused
by the suddenness of the death of the loved one.

When adolescents lose someone to an anticipatory death (e.g., a
terminal illness such as cancer or AIDS), they have more time to contemplate the impending loss and therefore more time to talk to and share
their feelings with the dying person. It is important to note, however,
that even when a loss is expected, there is no guarantee that the adolescent will actually prepare for the death. Most of the adolescents in our
bereavement groups who lost loved ones to terminal illnesses said they
felt that for them to accept the inevitability of the death was tantamount
to their losing hope. Also, they said, watching a loved one suffer from
a devastating illness had a detrimental effect on their healing process.
Many group members reported being haunted by memories and visions
of seeing a loved one suffer excruciating pain without their being able
to alleviate the dying person's misery.

Like those who lose a loved one to AIDS, adolescents who lose a
loved one to a violent death, such as homicide or suicide, may feel reluctant to acknowledge and discuss the cause of the death for fear of being
stigmatized and looked at in a negative light by their community.
Adolescents may feel conflicted by feelings of sadness and anger directed
at the person who died and also to anyone else they feel was somehow
responsible for the death. Feelings of revenge and hatred may cloud these
adolescents' thoughts as they attempt to make sense of a world that no
longer feels fair or secure. While trying to come to terms with incidents
of homicide in which the perpetrator is still at large, adolescents may find
themselves preoccupied with thoughts of avenging the death or an
obsession with seeing justice meted out. As a result, their feelings of
anxiety and helplessness may interrupt and delay their healing process.
In cases of losing a loved one to suicide, adolescents may be plagued by
unanswered questions, confusion over possibly misinterpreting signals
given by the deceased, and feelings of guilt and betrayal. Adolescents who
either witness a death or are first on the scene to find the body after a
homicide or suicide often suffer severe trauma. Events such as these may

leave adolescents numb and in shock and unable to process what they have seen or heard. Seeing as how these adolescents require an outlet through which they can identify and express their feelings, they may also benefit from professional assistance from a mental health practitioner.

Unfortunately, many adolescents who are in the dark as to the cause of one's death believe that the adults in their lives are not always truthful with them about the details of their loved one's death, such as how or when the person died. For their part, adults often worry that adolescents are "too young" to understand certain harsh realities; therefore, these well-meaning adults may try to shield them from pain. We at the CBP always encourage adults and caregivers to be honest about a death, to answer questions and not to lie. By doing so, they help adolescents to be trustful, to feel that they are an important part of their family, and to be free of feelings of stigmatization that might be brought on by the circumstances surrounding the death of their loved one.

Reactions of Other Family Members to the Death

The way adolescents grieve often has much to do with how their family grieves. Naturally, the entire family is affected by a death (Lehmann, Jimerson, & Gaasch, 2001). If a family avoids discussing the death of a loved one, they are either directly or indirectly sending their offspring the message that it is inappropriate, or not OK, to talk about the death. In adolescents, this restrained, almost nonexistent style of grieving may lead to feelings of isolation. Furthermore, many adolescents may fear that talking about the loved one will upset surviving family members. This reluctance of family members to communicate with each other will result in adolescents' keeping their feelings inside and therefore stunt their grieving process.

Families that discuss without reservation the loss of a loved one provide adolescents with the means to grieve openly and cling to and integrate into their lives the memories of the deceased. This open style of family grieving (like the closed style discussed in the previous paragraph) is a product of many factors, including the family's tradition of cultural and religious views on death and dying and the reaction and support of the community that surrounds them. The family's culture also acts as a determinant in the family's grieving process, including how long the family grieves the death of a loved one, the number and types of rituals and ceremonies it practices, and the overall nature of the family's degree of expressiveness.

Prior Loss Experiences and Multiple Losses

An adolescent who has endured a prior loss or multiple losses may experience new losses in different ways. Some adolescents may appear to be sensitized to grief and treat new losses without much outward emotion, although they are actually repressing their feelings as a way to cope. Others, on the other hand, may become despondent and fearful that everyone around them may die. This fear may in turn adversely affect their ability to form new attachments with people. Some adolescents may be able to accept prior or multiple losses simply as a fact of life and consequently use them as a learning experience that teaches them to value communication and the ups and downs of life.

Community Mortality Patterns

The experience a community has with death is also an important factor in the grieving process. A community that faces high mortality rates due to terminal diseases, such as AIDS and cancer, or acts of violence may be better prepared and more open about assisting bereaved populations. In East Harlem, many youth-based organizations are aware that bereaved adolescents have special needs and are interested in providing them with needed education and counseling services. Providing these services, however, requires a commitment and a general openness and willingness to talk about death and dying. Adolescents who live in these types of communities and attend schools in which death is discussed find that their healing process is enhanced, in contrast to adolescents who live in communities in which death is considered taboo.

Different Personalities

As we have learned firsthand, all adolescents come equipped with their own unique personalities and temperaments, and this fact greatly affects the grieving process. No two adolescents are identical. Within the context of a group, we are able to see the individual strengths and challenges facing each group member. Individual factors, such as adolescents' differing levels of emotional maturity and stability, their ability to express themselves, and their ability to form attachments and connections with others, greatly influence the grieving process.

Social Support Systems

Adolescents with strong social support systems normally receive more help, encouragement, and understanding during the grieving process. Those who lack this support are usually unable to talk to their peers and family members and therefore lack much-needed opportunities for healing. Some of the adolescents we have worked with have said that they feel they need to be strong in front of their family and not let their true feelings show. This belief leads them to feel more isolated and alone.

Many of these adolescents feel that they received more support directly after the death, but also believe that that support quickly began to fade until it disappeared altogether. When we conduct our initial intake with adolescents, we ask them about their social support network and about who they feel comfortable talking with about their loss. We are repeatedly surprised at how few people these adolescents feel comfortable talking with; this problem thus reinforces their need and desire to join a bereavement group.

Consequences of Stress

Many aspects of adolescents' lives change after a death. This change adds more stress to their daily lives and therefore requires adjustments to an already difficult healing process. Some common stressors that affect adolescents who are grieving include the following (Kandt, 1994):

> *The need to move elsewhere:* As a result of a death, an adolescent may have to move to another household or another neighborhood. This usually means that the adolescent ends up living farther away from friends and possibly with extended family who are virtual strangers. Some adolescents also find themselves having to change schools, which can be a huge stressor.
>
> *Financial difficulties:* The loss of a loved one may mean the loss of financial security for the family. As a result, an adolescent may be forced to get a job or take on extra responsibilities around the house so that other family members can work.
>
> *Academic difficulties:* Many adolescents face added academic stressors after a death, most often because they have fallen behind in their studies or are unable to concentrate and complete their assignments.
>
> *Relationship problems:* The stress of losing a loved one often places added strain on existing relationships. Adolescents often report feeling angry and arguing with their parents, siblings, and friends out of frustration and despair.
>
> *Health problems:* Many adolescents experience physical problems after the death of a loved one. The changes and stress that accompany such a staggering loss often cause adolescents to forget about taking care of themselves and simply ignore their health.

WHAT GRIEVING ADOLESCENTS TEACH US ABOUT THEIR EMOTIONAL, BEHAVIORAL, AND PHYSICAL PROBLEMS

Although there is extensive literature and research that deals with how adolescents grieve, most of what we at the CBP have learned has originated from the adolescents themselves. Through extensive one-on-one interviews and group discussions, our group members have relayed vital information to us about what they experienced after a death and how their behavior changed as a result of their loss. This information has helped us immeasurably as we strive to better understand adolescent grief reactions.

Sleep Disturbances

Many adolescents report changes in their sleeping patterns after the death of a loved one. Some are unable to sleep at night and suffer from insomnia. As a result, during the day they often experience fatigue and difficulty with concentration. Others find themselves sleeping excessively. Many adolescents report having dreams and nightmares about the person who died. Some are comforted by dreams of their loved ones, feeling closer and more connected to them, whereas others feel disturbed or scared by such occurrences. Nightmares leave many adolescents frazzled and anxious about returning to sleep, thus worsening their insomnia.

Changes in Eating Habits

Many adolescents are affected by grief in ways that are obvious to friends and family. Their distress may manifest itself through a range of physical behaviors, including upset stomach, nausea, diarrhea, constipation, and vomiting. These symptoms should be monitored by adults because they can lead to serious disorders, such as anorexia and bulimia. Parents and guardians should be aware of any changes in an adolescent's eating habits: increased or decreased appetite, hoarding of certain foods, pronounced weight loss or weight gain, noticeable physical changes, aversion and avoidance of certain foods, or frequent vomiting episodes (DSM-IV, 1994). A grieving adolescent in emotional pain may resort to these and other destructive behaviors in an attempt to regain some control.

Academic Indifference

The majority of the adolescent grievers in our CBP bereavement groups experience pronounced distraction and disturbances in concentration following the death of a loved one. They find that their attention spans are diminished, making it more difficult to stay focused in class and complete their homework assignments. Others report feeling too angry to care about school or simply too overwhelmed by their grief experience to be able to fulfill their academic responsibilities. As a result, many adolescent grievers suffer from poor grades and test scores, a lack of organization, and incomplete work. Many of these adolescents become habitually tardy to and excessively absent from school. With the adolescents' permission, we often find it helpful to talk with teachers about the needs of adolescents in grief and solicit their suggestions on how to help them maneuver their responsibilities during this difficult time. We always make it a point to remind the teachers to keep the information confidential.

Disturbances in Social Functioning and Peer Relationships

Many adolescents we work with have stated that their death experience left them feeling different and isolated from many of their friends. Adolescents often feel major changes after they experience a death. To them, the world is no longer the same place they thought it was. Spending time with peers whose world is still the same can be a frustrating and lonely experience. Feeling alone in their struggle of loss, adolescents often suffer socially and may feel awkward reintegrating into their peer groups and classroom circles. Because adolescence is primarily a time of peer group interactions, this feeling of alienation can be especially devastating to adolescent grievers.

Feelings of Withdrawal

Adolescents experience a range of emotions after a death. Some exhibit signs of withdrawal as well as a general loss of interest in daily activities. These symptoms may be considered risk factors for depression and suicide and call for close attention from the adults in these adolescents' lives. Parents and guardians may find it necessary to seek professional help.

Crying and Tearfulness

Although crying is a normal expression of grief, it is not an essential component of grieving. Not all adolescents are comfortable crying in public—they may feel shy and awkward or may feel more at ease crying in private. Many adolescents are afraid to cry because it makes them feel vulnerable; thus they may actively try not to cry. In our CBP groups, we make it clear that crying is a normal expression of grief and perfectly acceptable as long as the adolescent feels comfortable crying. Regardless of whether members cry, we encourage the group to be supportive of all group members.

Physical Complaints

As mentioned earlier, adolescents often experience a range of physical reactions after a death. The emotional energy required during the grieving process often tires them, both physically and emotionally. Many adolescents report a general feeling of tiredness, whereas others feel fatigued to the point of having difficulty functioning. This exhaustion may lead to a slightly compromised immune system for some adolescents, making them more prone to illness. Other common physical responses to grief include headaches, stomachaches and other gastrointestinal problems, unexplained muscle and bone aches, shortness of breath, quickened heartbeat, and dizziness (The Dougy Center, 1999).

Pronounced Anger or Defiance

After the death of a loved one, adolescents may exhibit pronounced anger and physical aggression. They may find themselves readily becoming involved in physical fights and rebellious behavior targeted at authority figures. Such behavior by adolescents may indicate an effort to take control over some aspect of their lives and may also serve as a protective mechanism as they purposely act out in an effort to alienate adults and peers.

Regressive Behavior

Some adolescents in grief, especially younger ones, exhibit regressive behavior. Adolescents who are grieving often exhibit childlike behaviors of both a physical and an emotional nature. Some common regressive behaviors include thumb sucking, timidity or shyness about taking part in everyday activities, bed-wetting, altered speech patterns, and exaggerated attachments to surviving family and friends (The Dougy Center, 1999).

Becoming "Mini-Adults"

Some adolescents take on excessive responsibilities after a loved one dies. As a result of changes in family composition, they begin to feel obligated to fill the role that the deceased played in the family. Some adolescents look for jobs so they can earn money to help secure the financial situation of the family; others decide to take on more domestic roles, such as cooking, cleaning, and caring for younger siblings.

Activity and Play

For some adolescents, engaging in various activities helps to alleviate their grieving. These pursuits may include participating in sports, spending more time with friends, and engaging in an assortment of new hobbies. Sometimes parents and guardians express concern that their children are able to play and continue with their routine after a death, afraid that their adolescents are overcompensating as a means of suppressing their grief. In fact, play and activity can offer adolescents a more positive outlet for their grief rather than talking to others about their feelings. As is often the case, adolescents may not be ready to talk about their feelings.

Nightmares, Dreams, and Visions

As noted earlier, it is not uncommon for adolescents to report having vivid dreams and nightmares involving the deceased. Some adolescents also see visions of their loved one or experience other unexplained sounds or smells that are reminiscent of the person who died. Many of these adolescents feel relieved to discover that they are not the only ones to experience such events.

Cultural, Religious, and Spiritual Beliefs and Traditions

For some adolescents, their faith and belief in a higher being can be a comfort to them as they attempt to make sense of their feelings of loss. Special rituals or ceremonies can provide opportunities for families to grieve together and incorporate the deceased into their lives. However, for those adolescents who are struggling to make sense of their own beliefs, participating in religious services can sometimes hamper their grieving; they often feel that these services are inauthentic and, as a result, overwhelming.

WHEN TO INTERVENE: CHARACTERISTIC GRIEVING PATTERNS AND WARNING SIGNS

Parents and youth workers often approach us, concerned about an adolescent who is grieving in an "abnormal" way. They may be concerned about an adolescent who is "still" upset after many months or one who never seems upset at all. Although we do not believe in the existence of "abnormal grief," we do recognize that some adolescents display grief patterns that require further attention or professional help. In fact, should any of the grief reactions described in the previous section show little or no sign of improving, we recommend that parents and guardians express their concern to their children and have a talk with them about other possible steps that can be taken to help them during their grieving. Aside from—or in addition to—bereavement groups, adolescents may benefit from individual and family counseling.

Although there is no set framework that dictates when certain adolescent grief responses call out for professional assistance, the following behaviors should be monitored for further assessment and evaluation (Kandt, 1994):

> *Adolescents whose symptoms of grief are prolonged and show little indication of subsiding.* These symptoms may be of a phys-

ical nature, such as persistent headaches or fatigue, or they may be of an emotional nature, such as persistent and intense feelings of guilt, anger, or revenge.

Adolescents who appear to be suppressing their grief reaction, thereby delaying their healing process. In our intake interviews, we ask our adolescents if they ever find themselves denying that the death has occurred or pretending that the loved one is still alive. If so, further professional intervention is needed.

Adolescents whose grief reaction appears to be disabling and thus interferes with daily function at school, at home, and with peers. For example, adolescents may continue to have chronic panic or anxiety attacks that pull them away from school responsibilities. Chronic depression is also a disabling condition that often interferes with normal daily function.

Adolescents whose grief response is continually expressed through behaviors that may be unsafe or unhelpful. In these situations, adolescents may engage in excessive drug use or sexual activity (especially unsafe sexual activity) or other risk-taking behaviors; they may also, for example, exhibit eating disorders.

Depression and Suicide

Adolescents sometimes exhibit severe signs of depression after a death. Although certain emotional, behavioral, and physical symptoms of depression—which were discussed previously—are to be expected in the wake of a death, a chronic display of such symptoms may be an indication that professional intervention is needed.

Some of the adolescents in our groups have mentioned a desire to "be with their loved one" or a wish to be dead so that they can be together with the deceased. Although we have found remarks such as these to be rather common and not always examples of suicidal ideation, all such statements or actions made in reference to suicide should be taken seriously. *All adolescents whose words or behaviors suggest suicidal ideation should be asked outright whether they have any thoughts, wishes, or plans to hurt or kill themselves.* It is also important to discuss any threats of suicide they may have made or to talk about past attempts at suicide, if applicable. Whenever we mention this topic while conducting training sessions, someone will invariably ask if mentioning suicide to adolescents—especially to those who are not thinking about it—will automatically start them thinking about the idea. What we explain to the questioner is that, at least in this case, the power of suggestion is a myth. Suicidal ideation is rarely an impulsive event; rather, it is one that has already taken root. Behaviors and comments that may be warning signs of suicidal ideation include closure-type conversations in which adolescents talk about goodbyes and thank-yous, giving away their possessions, the concept of death or wanting to die, sudden changes in personality, and increased risk-taking conduct.

In our years of running the CBP, we have referred quite a few adolescents for suicidal evaluation at our local hospitals. It is imperative always to prepare a plan of action in the event that adolescents exhibit suicidal tendencies. This plan should include the participation of parents or guardians and other important contact people at the host agency. The adolescent must be told from the outset that disclosure of suicidal thoughts cannot be kept confidential and always warrants a plan of action. Facilitators should never promise to keep it a secret. Adolescents will react in different ways when referred for suicidal evaluation at a hospital: Some are relieved, but others become angry and feel betrayed. It is vital to follow up with adolescents to find out what they are feeling and thinking. It is also imperative that facilitators have ready at all times the necessary hospital contact and suicide hotline information. In addition, they must be aware that not all hospitals have adolescent psychiatric units.

CHAPTER
2

Groups as Effective Tools for Grieving Adolescents

People who are unfamiliar with the Children's Bereavement Project (CBP) often ask us why we choose to facilitate groups for adolescents in grief, rather than rely on individual or family therapy. Although some adolescents may indeed benefit from individual counseling or a combination of other methods, we have found that groups offer adolescents many avenues of healing that other treatment methods do not.

Groups bring adolescents together, where they are able to share their experiences, determine what they have in common, make connections, work through conflict by taking a healthful and safe approach, and provide and receive support. Most important, groups provide the opportunity for mutual aid, which has been defined simply as "people helping each other as they think things through" (Steinberg, 1997, p. xv).

At the CBP, it has been our experience that mutual aid bereavement groups provide an adequate sense of identity and affiliation to grieving adolescents, many of whom start out feeling different and misunderstood and are fearful of being marginalized by their peer groups. If a mutual aid group is to be successful in its mission, all of its members must know both explicitly and implicitly that they are needed and valued and that the interactions and relationships between and among them are vital components of the group process. It is clear to us that by joining and experiencing mutual aid groups, adolescents regain a sense of belonging, competence, and hope as they grieve the death of a loved one. By highlighting the attributes and benefits afforded adolescents in grief, this chapter provides information that is invaluable to those who wish to create a warm, successful mutual aid climate.

HEALING ATTRIBUTES OF BEREAVEMENT GROUPS

Bereavement groups comprise many therapeutic attributes. As a result, they provide an assortment of opportunities for group facilitators to help adolescents journey through the grieving process. Many of these attributes, along with the successes they have fostered, have been observed and documented by many social group work theorists over the years (Malekoff, 1997; Northen, 1988; Steinberg, 1997). Included in this chapter are a number of positive group qualities that have been brought to light by Northen (1988) and others and subsequently applied to adolescents in grief.

Enabling Grieving Adolescents to Anticipate Mutual Support

This stage of life is a time when adolescents begin to gravitate toward their peer groups and away from their families for support. These groups provide not only peer support, but also support from the adult group facilitator who joins them. This supportive environment lessens anxiety and allows for healthy communication and positive risk-taking behaviors. Therefore, bereavement groups are an ideal setting for adolescents to be able to provide and receive support in a safe place. Many of our adolescents report feeling "good" and "proud" that they are able to join a bereavement group, knowing that they are helping themselves and their peers at the same time.

Providing a Cohesive Environment and a Sense of Community for Adolescents

Within mutual aid groups, members make a commitment to each other and therefore to the purpose and goals of the group. As a result, group members are able to feel supported and understood, thus facilitating their sense of connection to each other. In bereavement groups, all members share a common experience—the loss of a loved one—and this bond serves as the foundation of an environment in which cohesiveness can develop naturally. This togetherness enables group members to feel as though they are a part of a vital and important community.

Encouraging Bereaved Adolescents to Develop High-Quality Relationships with One Another

Groups provide the opportunity for in-depth relationships to develop between members. Bereavement groups offer a structured setting wherein members can count on being helped to take positive risks simultaneously, thus allowing for even stronger relationships to be created and prosper. Group members observe each other, as well as the group facilitator, and learn how to be supportive and empathic toward one another, thus strengthening the bonds within the group.

Helping Adolescents to Discover That They Are Not Alone

Groups provide adolescents with the opportunity to understand the significance of the common bonds between them. Bereavement groups are created with the intention of helping adolescents to recognize common experiences and feelings shared by their members. Although their individual experiences are unique, all members have experienced loss and therefore share similar feelings and struggles that help the group to bond. Discovering that their feelings are not uncommon helps to begin an important healing process for these adolescents. Some shy adolescents, for example, may decide that it is all right for them to discuss a number of concerns that they have always had, yet up until now, have feared sharing with others. By listening to their peers bring these "dark secrets" out into the open, other reluctant adolescents begin to feel a sense of relief and comfort, secure in the knowledge that they now have a safety net to protect them from their fears of alienation. Participation in a bereavement group can also ease fears of stigma often connected to death, such as might be felt by adolescents who disclose that a loved one died of AIDS (Schoeman & Kreitzman, 1997). Group members soon realize that they are all pretty much in the same boat and therefore can begin to feel less alone and more a part of the group.

Helping Grieving Adolescents to Rediscover Lost Feelings of Hope

Bereavement groups make it possible for adolescents to gain a sense of renewed hope for themselves following the death of a loved one. By their very nature, these groups bring the grieving process into clear focus, enabling adolescents to see that other people have had similar experiences and are coping successfully. As a result, grieving adolescents are given the opportunity to share their own methods of coping and at the same time learn the coping methods used by others. Group members share a range of feelings, from regret and fear to optimism and hope. By expressing methods of coping, adolescents discover that hope is on everyone's mind and represents a crucial aspect of working through the grieving process. They soon begin to feel comfortable and trusting when they note that the group is assessing their feelings of grief and working to help them regain a sense of hope by using different methods, including group activities, to help them through this difficult time in their lives.

Encouraging Adolescents to Help One Another

Groups provide members with an opportunity not only to receive support, but also to show support for their fellow members. It is a process that strengthens everyone's sense of self and personal identity by underscoring the importance of encouragement. In fact, many adolescents state that they join a bereavement group because they want to share their feelings and be able to help other adolescents like themselves. At the CBP, for example, we have often witnessed members sharing the experiences they have had with depression and suicidal thoughts, offering personal accounts with the intention of helping others who may be feeling the same way. These adolescents feel good about themselves and others when they know that their insight and encouragement are sought and valued.

Providing Group Members with New Skills and Knowledge

Bereavement groups provide members with an opportunity to learn new information and skills and to acquire knowledge. Adolescents learn important communication and interpersonal skills within a group setting as well as important values, such as patience, acceptance, and understanding. In bereavement groups, adolescents are able to share their own coping styles and insights about grief, life, and death, thus lending important thoughts and skills to the group. As mentioned earlier, these adolescents are able to share ideas and to recognize together that they have in common many life experiences from which there is always something to be learned.

Providing a Safe Outlet for Discussing and Releasing Pent-Up Emotions

Groups offer members the opportunity to discuss their experiences and release their pent-up emotions. In the process, adolescents discover that they don't feel as nervous as they thought they would and also find that they feel increasingly confident the more they cooperate with the other members and the group facilitator. In bereavement groups, members often feel a tremendous sense of relief at finally having a safe place to discuss their grieving and safe people with whom they can share their life stories—in other words, people who have just as much at stake as they do by sharing their experiences. Whether the experiences they share are positive or negative, the most important point is that all group members are free to share them.

Convincing Adolescents to Approach rather than to Avoid

Many adolescents decide to join bereavement groups because they are seeking support, even though their experiences with death may have left them fearful of trusting new people and new experiences. Thus these adolescents are volunteering to enter a struggle that involves balancing their desire to approach a bereavement group with their inclination to avoid it. The opportunity that this gives them, coupled with their ability to work through such conflicts, is one of the most impressive attributes of the mutual aid group. Adolescents who join the group learn to see conflict not as the enemy, but rather as a healthy and valued component of their personal growth.

As the group sessions continue, the facilitator models empathy, acceptance, and care, and the group members soon acquire the ability to demonstrate these traits to one another (Northen, 1988). Within this caring setting, the group offers members the opportunity to "re-experience dysfunctional patterns and relationships and to work through these dynamics in a safe and supportive environment" (Malekoff, 1997, p. 40). Members can use the group environment to explore issues in a healthy manner and to think of and strive to achieve appropriate goals regarding practicing and addressing certain behaviors. For example, group members who have never spoken about their loved one's death can take small steps to address this issue within the safety of the group.

Providing Group Members with an Environment That Allows for Reality Checks

Within the group setting, adolescents are not only able, but also encouraged, to confront and support each other regarding unsafe behaviors or exaggerations or distortions of fact. Adolescents tend to be more comfortable and more open to listening to their peers in a supportive environment such as a bereavement group. Members may challenge certain actions that they may disagree with, or they may dispute unrealistic feelings, such as denial or displaced anger. This freedom to speak their minds opens the door to discussion of risky behavior and may, in the end, help to minimize the number of questionable or objectionable situations in which some of the group members may find themselves.

Another advantage that adolescents have in working through their grief in bereavement groups is that they can feel unabashedly free to address some of their own various acting-out behaviors and grief-related feelings. For example, a member may feel that she caused her grandmother's heart attack because, at some earlier date, she had silently wished that her grandmother would die. The group can help her to work through her feelings of guilt and self-blame by convincing her that it was not she who actually caused her grandmother to die.

Offering Adolescents Structure, Limits, and Consistency

All groups require a certain amount of structure to ensure that healthy and positive group norms are developed. From the beginning stage of the group, members learn that certain norms and expectations are required of them so that the goals and purpose of the group can be realized and group members can, at the same time, feel safe and comfortable. Any action or behavior that is detrimental to the safety of the group members or the welfare of the group as a whole is monitored and addressed by the group members and the group facilitator. It is crucial that group members work together as they all share the spotlight and contribute their stories. For the bereavement group to be a success, all the group members must work to maintain a safe environment in which personal feelings and experiences can be shared openly and securely. The group should therefore have structure that puts limits on behavior and ensures that every time it meets, its members will expect and experience consistency.

Allowing Adolescents to Practice and Develop New Roles and Responsibilities

Groups offer members countless opportunities for individual growth and development and healing. They also provide adolescents with the opportunity to utilize their individual strengths within the group setting and to create and develop new roles for themselves. For example, group members may develop new leadership and assertiveness skills as well as a variety of communication skills that subsequently enable them to practice new ways of expressing themselves within the group. In bereavement groups, as the safety of the group becomes evident, members will become more comfortable sharing their stories and begin to act toward others in a supportive manner so that they, too, can be comfortable in sharing themselves.

IMPORTANCE OF THE MUTUAL AID APPROACH TO GROUPS

In a group environment, the opportunity and need for mutual aid last from the time group members enter the room till the time they leave. Mutual aid involves the following: having adolescents share information with one another and their facilitator; lending support when they see that it is needed; and accepting acknowledgment, understanding, nods of approval, and light touches on the shoulder and even hugs. During the intake interview, it is important that the group facilitator discuss with each potential group member that this type of supportive touching between members (and facilitator) is both normal and acceptable, as long as permission is both asked for and granted. For example, a member who is crying may be asked by fellow group members if a hug at that moment would be helpful. This question enables the member to indicate whether this type of supportive touching is comfortable, and it also helps the group to understand that every member has his or her own comfort level when it comes to this type of behavior.

Mutual aid involves cultivating self-advocacy and change; taking positive risks; and safely exploring commonalities, differences, and difficulties. Most important, mutual aid centers on using the group forum to help others by encouraging group members to contribute their thoughts, experiences, feelings, and beliefs and to absorb what they can from hearing everyone else's thoughts, experiences, feelings, and beliefs. Whenever they enter this environment, group members bring with them their singular experiences, which eventually affect the individual growth and development of the other adolescents and their group experience as a whole.

With all the potential benefits of helping adolescents to grieve in group settings, one might wonder why every group does not yield the same successful results. During our training sessions, for example, bereavement group facilitators often complain about the difficult and unsuccessful groups they have "led," describing disorganized and chaotic groups in which the members are impolite, lazy, averse to listening, and unsupportive of one another. Unfortunately, the positive effects of mutual aid do not spontaneously emerge once a group of adolescents gathers together in a room for a group bereavement meeting. It is simply impracticable to give facilitators a handout titled "Creating Mutual Aid Groups" and expect them to achieve immediate results. However, many social group work theorists believe that all groups have "the potential for mutual aid," as long as certain conditions coexist within the group setting (Steinberg 1997, p. xviii). According to Steinberg, ideally a number of conditions should coexist if successful mutual aid is to occur.

One important condition that must exist if mutual aid is to be effective is that group facilitators be experienced and expert role models. Using specific skills that must be acquired over time, group facilitators play a central role in developing a mutual aid environment, especially in the beginning stage of the group. Facilitators assume the vital role of recognizing and capitalizing on "mutual aid moments" and helping members to interact and communicate with each other. For example, by modeling appropriate communication techniques, facilitators teach the adolescents in the group to speak directly to one another, rather than to speak primarily to the facilitator in a dialogue format. Within mutual aid settings, facilitators are not viewed as the only ones in the "helper roles"—rather, facilitators share their authority so that the individual skills of the members can be used to benefit the group as a whole (Steinberg, 1997). The literature makes it a point to describe the role of the practitioner in this way—as "worker" rather than as "leader" (Steinberg, 1997; Trecker, 1955). For our purposes, however, we will call the worker the *facilitator*. Although facilitators are the ones who have gained much expertise and invaluable experience in the field of bereavement work with adolescents, the foundation of mutual aid is underpinned by all members—not just by facilitators, but by adolescent grievers as well—all of whom bring their uniqueness to the group. In mutual aid bereavement groups, as in other mutual aid groups, facilitators help to promote and ensure a safe climate in which members are able to share freely and without embarrassment their loss experiences with one another.

It bears repeating that for mutual aid to develop properly, group members must have the capacity to communicate not only with one another, but also with the facilitator—and in a variety of ways as well. For example, it is well known that useful, valid participation and communication can occur both verbally and nonverbally. Some mutual aid theorists feel that what is referred to as the *free-floating* communication style is the only one that truly fosters a climate of mutual aid (Middleman & Wood, 1990a). In the free-floating style, members are encouraged to speak when they have something to say about the subject being discussed. What this style succeeds in accomplishing is to allow members to interact directly with one another while carrying on a spontaneous discussion at the same time. Meanwhile, the facilitator must help members to be respectful of one another and to remind them not to interrupt when someone else is speaking. At the CBP, we use this free-floating form of communication in our bereavement groups: (a) Group members are encouraged to speak when they have something to contribute; (b) they are not required to raise their hands before speaking; and (c) both their verbal and nonverbal styles of communication are recognized by the facilitator. We feel that other methods of communication, such as instructing members to take turns speaking or urging them to speak individually with the facilitator, limit the development of mutual aid.

Another important condition that must exist in a bereavement group if mutual aid is to be successful is an environment in which group members feel comfortable sharing their thoughts and feelings regarding the group's content and direction. Adolescents should always have the freedom to express themselves, as long as they do so in a respectful manner. The climate of a mutual aid group should feel safe enough for members to take positive risks, while at the same time recognizing the importance of listening with sensitivity and an open mind. In the process, facilitators must share their authority so that decisions made within the group reflect every member's input. In bereavement groups, members have the advantage of being able to work together to decide what topics they want to discuss and how much they want to share.

One necessary condition of mutual aid is to bring people together in such a way that they are able to focus on a common cause. This condition helps members to connect with each other so that they are able both to provide and to receive support. If mutual aid is to develop, a clear group purpose is imperative. Although the individual goals of members may change as the needs of the group change as a whole, these goals should always reflect the common cause that connects all group members. For example, in the beginning stage of a bereavement group, members may wish to discuss their stories without sharing their feelings, whereas in the middle or ending stage of the group, as they begin to feel more comfortable, they may wish not only to discuss their stories but also to share their feelings about their stories. However adolescents go about it, they must make sure that the good of the group always take precedence: Adolescents, all of whom have lost a loved one, come together, seeking to become part of a supportive environment in which they can both provide and receive support.

A major advantage of concentrating on a common goal is that group members cannot help but remember that, although they are grieving, they are grieving with others in the midst of a mutual aid environment. As a result, they become motivated to try new ways of thinking and being. Activities within the group, such as those that center on art, dialogue, and role play, fortify them by further generating their creative expression.

SIGNIFICANCE OF MUTUAL AID

It is only natural to focus on and discuss at length the conditions necessary for creating a mutual aid climate. Especially for adolescents who are partaking of the benefits of a bereavement group, the significance of mutual aid cannot be underestimated. These adolescents, many of whom have seen their lives altered as a result of the loss of a loved one, must be allowed to grieve in a climate that fosters togetherness. For them not only to survive, but also to thrive, they must be able to depend on the comfort that a climate of give-and-take provides them.

Helping Adolescents to Understand What They Bring to the Group

A true mutual aid environment helps group members to identify the individual strengths that they bring to the group (Steinberg, 1997). Compared to a pathology-based model, in which most of the emphasis is placed on one's weaknesses or deficits, a model that is based on mutual aid emphasizes identifying and nurturing one's strengths. Within a mutual aid environment, it is assumed that all group members possess individual strengths, which are first identified within the group environment and then developed and reinforced over time. In addition, the mutual aid model strives to find the strength in group members' personal traits. As a result, all group members in a mutual aid system come to the group with individual resources that are then used for the benefit of the group as a whole. In the typical adolescent bereavement groups discussed in this book, members learn to acknowledge and credit each other for qualities such as positive risk taking, willingness to share, supportive behavior, and understanding and empathizing with fellow group members.

Providing an Opportunity for Group Members to Problem Solve

Mutual aid affords group members a vehicle for effective problem solving. Because adolescents are eager and usually efficient at offering suggestions for strengthening the group, members strive to work together to solve conflicts that arise from time to time.

Helping Adolescents to Notice Attributes They Have in Common

Mutual aid enables group members to identify and understand the range of commonalities that connect them and their experiences, needs, feelings, and goals. Consequently, group members are encouraged to take on more leadership tasks and decision-making responsibilities (Steinberg, 1997; Middleman & Wood, 1990b). The group facilitator plays a key role in assisting adolescents with the group-building process as well as other aspects of mutual aid.

Enabling and Encouraging Adolescents to Share with One Another

Mutual aid helps group members to identify their own experiences, knowledge, and feelings so that they can share them with the rest of the group. Bereavement group members practice reflecting upon and talking about their experiences; when they do, other members are also able and free to react by sharing their own experiences. This process is the direct opposite of advice giving, which is counterproductive to the development of mutual aid. Instead of being told, "You should do this," group members connect by listening to each other's stories and then reacting normally, without feeling defensive or patronized.

Examples of Mutual Aid in Action:
Seeking and Finding Help from Bereavement Groups

▷ When he was 8 years old, Matt witnessed his father's being shot and killed in a crossfire. He joined the bereavement group to have a safe place to explore his unresolved feelings about his loss. Midway through the group, the East Harlem community was stunned by the suicide of a woman, who threw herself off the roof of her building. The woman was Matt's mother, and the bereavement group was his salvation. Riddled with grief, he came to school for the sole purpose of joining and seeking support from his peers.

▷ When he was 5, Juan was being bullied by another child. As his mother tried to reason with the mother of the child who was bullying her son, she was brutally stabbed to death. Nine years later, in the bereavement group, Juan shared for the first time the overwhelming sense of guilt that had dominated his life ever since the horrific incident. As a result, he finally began to feel a sense of support and relief.

▷ When she returned home from summer camp just before entering the third grade, Vanessa went into shock when she was informed that her mother had committed suicide while she was gone. That fall, when Vanessa told her classmates about the suicide, her story was met with laughter from many of her peers. From that day on, Vanessa vowed never to tell another person how her mother died. It wasn't until she joined a bereavement group in the eighth grade that she felt secure enough to share her secret. The group's positive and supportive responses helped her to rethink the stigma she had connected with her mother's death and made her realize that there actually were people who did care.

CHAPTER
3

Planning a Bereavement Group for Adolescents

The CBP began with a single idea about conducting groups in schools for adolescents who are involved in the grieving process. We discussed the matter with principals, teachers, parents, and most important, adolescents, to gather their thoughts on having bereavement programs in their schools. Taking into account what it would mean to have their support and the resources necessary to get such bereavement groups off the ground, we began to visualize what our groups would look like.

Keeping all of these variables in mind, we then began to consider a number of important questions we would need to answer before beginning a bereavement group for adolescents, including the following:

What would be the purpose of the group?

Who would want to join the group?

How long and how often would the group meet?

What would we do once we got the group together?

How would we handle the inevitable crises that would arise, and how many of these unique situations would we be likely to encounter?

Pondering these questions galvanized us to begin shaping and creating our program and proved to be a vital tool for helping to make the program a success. Our determination to think ahead and prepare for the unknown involved a thought process known simply as pre-group planning. To that end, this chapter outlines vital information on planning a bereavement group for adolescents.

Planning is probably the most crucial element of group development because it is what guides the group facilitator's thoughts and decisions. It is also an ongoing process that evolves with the group. Thoughtful and comprehensive planning can minimize the negative consequences often attributed to poor planning—namely, high attrition, irregular attendance, low cohesiveness, poor motivation, and a lack of successful outcomes (Northen, 1988; Malekoff, 1997). Too often we hear about groups disintegrating for reasons that possibly could have been avoided had proper planning taken place. For example, adolescents' questioning why they are in the group, a lack of resources or adequate space, or a habit of just winging the day's activity and discussion can all lead to a group's demise. So how does one take the idea of running a bereavement group and transform it into a well-thought-out reality that best reflects the needs of a particular group of adolescents?

Within the field of social work, a number of models have been developed to help guide the facilitator through the pre-group planning stage. Roselle Kurland (1978, 1982) has developed a model for pre-group planning that consists of seven components: need, purpose, social/agency context, composition, structure, content, and pre-group contact. Her model consists of important aspects for the facilitator to consider when making decisions about planning the group and is intended to be used as a guide rather than a checklist. Depending on the type and nature of a particular group, certain components of the model may carry more importance than others during the planning stages of a group. What follows is based on our experience with planning bereavement groups and incorporates elements of Kurland's pre-group planning model as well as other aspects of planning.

WHY CONDUCT A BEREAVEMENT GROUP? ASSESSING THE NEED

In the past, bereavement groups have been formed for a variety of reasons:

1. A large number of adolescents have suffered losses and are feeling isolated.
2. The community has recently suffered a major loss.
3. A public or national loss has triggered personal grief reactions in adolescents.
4. The community faces high mortality rates due to illness or violence.
5. Adolescents have few or no outlets through which to express their grief.
6. Grieving adolescents are expressing themselves in unhealthy ways (e.g., through aggression, violence, truancy).

Our decision to inaugurate bereavement groups for adolescents was spurred by the overwhelming need we observed in East Harlem middle and junior high schools. Our sense of urgency was confirmed when we sat down to talk with school personnel and adolescents about their needs. Conducting a "needs assessment" is vital when planning a bereavement group—it offers us the opportunity to determine whether conducting a bereavement group is likely to satisfy the needs that adolescents feel they have.

What Are the General Needs of Adolescents?

Of course, the answer to this question depends a great deal on the particulars of the target population in your particular area. Factors such as age, developmental status, ethnic and cultural background, individual personality, community profile, and other sociocultural and environmental factors all affect the needs of adolescents. Therefore, it is well worth it to have periodic discussions with adolescents about their needs and ideas; in addition to their individual differences, they also are constantly changing and evolving. We have spent countless hours speaking with the members of our groups about what they think they need as adolescents. Although impossible to summarize in total, here are some of the things they have told us over time: They feel they need to be listened to, to feel respected, to be taken seriously, and to be able to trust others. They also need safe places to hang out, space to figure out who they are, time with their friends, time to have fun and goof around, a chance to prove they can be responsible, room to make mistakes and to learn from them, and adults who believe in them and are willing to help.

As group facilitators, we would add the following to this very important list: that adolescents need limits, dreams, reality checks, hugs (again, with prior permission), role models of all types, books, hope for the future, confidentiality, fun, and advocates. They need to be excited about learning, to develop goals by themselves, to determine their own interests and strengths, to deal with their struggles, to be accepted for their individuality, and to have an opportunity to share their life stories. Facilitators, meanwhile, must also ask themselves questions: What do the adolescents in your area feel they need? What do you as facilitator feel they need? Would heading a bereavement program meet some of these needs?

What Are the Specific Needs of Grieving Adolescents in Your Area?

What are the needs of the adolescents in your area who are in the process of grieving? Again, the answer to this question will depend largely on the particulars of your specific population of grieving adolescents. When we at the CBP sat down with our adolescents and asked them what they needed as grieving adolescents, this is some of what they told us: They felt they needed to know they were not alone, that they were supported, that they were able to express their feelings, that they were permitted time to feel sad, that they could seek and receive help with their schoolwork, and that they could count on adults to help them communicate with friends and family.

As group facilitators, we noted that they had other needs as well: a safe place to receive and provide support, tools to help them to identify and express their feelings about the death of their loved one, the opportunity to share their stories and learn about the commonalities and differences between their experiences and those of their peers, to remember the person who died, to learn that their feelings of grief are normal and that they have a right to grieve in their own unique way, to confront the reality of the death and its effect on their lives, and to ask questions about life and death—even if those questions cannot be answered. And so it remains: What do the grieving adolescents in your area feel they need? What do you as their facilitator feel they need? Will a bereavement group meet some of these needs?

EVALUATING THE HOST AGENCY

Although schools may be an ideal location to run bereavement groups (see chapter 6), they are by no means the only option. Given proper agency support and the necessary resources, a wide variety of settings can be used to host a bereavement group. Hospitals, churches, community-based centers, mental health clinics—all are viable locations for an adolescent bereavement group, as long as a few conditions are met.

First and foremost, the host agency should be committed to the needs of adolescents in grief. In fact, the notion of serving as the host of these bereavement groups should fall within the purview of the agency's mission statement and goals. The availability of requisite support and resources to facilitate the group's success, such as enough funds, staff, time, space, and materials, should be a given. Also, because support from the surrounding community is vital to the group's success, there should be no doubt that the following question will be answered in the affirmative: Will the community embrace a bereavement program and provide appropriate referrals?

In addition, every host agency needs to develop a crisis intervention plan that caters to the specifics of each adolescent population and each setting. Knowing how to handle situations that may involve depression and suicide and being able to provide appropriate referrals, if necessary, is imperative.

DETERMINING THE PURPOSE AND BENEFITS OF A BEREAVEMENT GROUP

At the CBP, we have found that adolescents join bereavement groups for a wide variety of reasons. Many adolescents say they want to be able to express their emotions and feel that, in such a setting, other group members will understand what they are going through. Others feel unable to talk about the loss of their loved one with family and friends and crave a supportive environment in which they may do so. Whatever their reasons for joining the group, all of the adolescents bring to the group their own hopes and experiences—some of which are universally felt, some of which are unique to them. To create a mutual aid environment in which all group members' needs can be met, the host agency needs to make its purpose clear to everyone involved in the group. Although each member will have his or her own hopes and expectations about what can be gained by participating in the group, the goals that group members will pursue together are referred to as the *group purpose*—the reason why members are in the group *together*. The group purpose reflects the "common cause" that connects all group members (Steinberg, 1997).

In a bereavement group, the group purpose may be stated as follows: to create a safe environment in which group members can provide and receive support regarding the death of a loved one. Although all members are naturally connected to this purpose, their individual goals may vary. One member may want to learn to express himself better, whereas another may need help minimizing her risky behavior. Because individual goals will change as the group evolves, it is vital for the group facilitator to solicit feedback from group members to determine whether the group purpose is being achieved. It is essential that the common cause always be clarified for every group member.

WHO SHOULD BE IN A BEREAVEMENT GROUP? ASSESSING GROUP COMPOSITION

Within the pre-group planning model, group composition is a very critical component to consider. In most groups, it is important to strike a balance between group members with respect to such variables as age, gender, ethnicity, socioeconomic status, educational background, previous group experience, and behavioral attributes. What we have discovered, however, is that the universality and common bond of the loss experience take precedence over normal group composition factors. Within the context of a mutual aid bereavement support group, adolescents realize that it does not really matter who is in the group, but rather that all group members have something in common.

Although there are no strict rules concerning who should or should not participate in a bereavement group, there are a number of different categories that a group facilitator should consider when determining the composition of a bereavement group. Following are some of the categories that guided us.

Number of Group Members

On the basis of our experience at the CBP, seven to eight adolescents in a group seems to be an ideal number. A larger group carries one major problem: There is not enough time that can be allotted for everyone to share because there are simply too many members in the group. However, because members sometimes drop out, recruiting about 10 students may eventually leave you with an ideal number. A group consisting of four to five adolescents can also work, yet it has been our experience that members of these smaller groups often yearn for a larger group so they can take comfort in knowing that more than just a few peers have had experiences with phenomena similar to their own.

Differences between Open and Closed Groups

An open group allows members to come and go as they please and for new members to join at any time. Open groups often continue indefinitely and do not have a set ending point. A closed group contains a prescreened number of group members who begin the group together and remain together until the end, without any new members being admitted after the group has begun meeting. Our experience leads us to believe that a closed format is better suited for an adolescent bereavement group. Our curriculum is founded on the concept of mutual aid, which evolves and develops most productively as members get to know each other and begin to feel comfortable trusting each other. This trust enables members to connect with their individual experiences and to begin to support each other. We feel that if new members were to join midway, the process of mutual aid could be disrupted and members might experience difficulty adjusting to this change.

A Single Facilitator or Co-Facilitators?

Bereavement groups can be facilitated by either one group facilitator or by two. At the CBP, we have always run our groups with a single facilitator. The principal benefits of this approach are that group members do not feel conflicted regarding the role of group facilitators, and group facilitators are able to develop their own style of interacting and enforcing group norms. This is not to say, however, that a co-facilitated group would not work. Having two group facilitators may lend group members more support as well as provide the facilitators with additional support for each other. Of course, co-leadership requires more prep time to address collaboration. (Further information on the qualities and responsibilities of the group facilitator is provided in chapter 4.)

Demographic and Descriptive Characteristics of Group Members

This section introduces and discusses the commonalities and differences that exist among group members with regard to the following factors: gender, grade/age, reading and writing proficiency, special education status, number of siblings, cultural and racial background, dialect, and religious background.

Gender

We have found that both boys and girls have no problems joining a bereavement group together. In the beginning of any group, it is normal for adolescents to observe the gender breakdown and to feel anxious about the idea of sharing or crying in front of members of the opposite sex. Unfortunately, many boys feel that they are not supposed to cry; many of the girls in our groups have verified this sentiment, noting that the men in their lives rarely cry. Yet, as group facilitators, we strongly emphasize that it is OK and normal for both girls *and* boys to cry. We discuss this problem during intake, and we talk about it again in the group sessions. By touching on this topic, we begin to counter some of the stereotypes and conditioned responses to crying. When the group and the group facilitator discuss this problem openly, group members begin to give and get support.

Grade/Age

Like mixed gender groups, mixed grade/age groups can be successful if, from the beginning stage of the group, it is discussed openly that death is universal and does not discriminate according to grade level or age. Despite that fact, mixing grades together in middle or junior high school can pose some difficulties. Seventh and eighth graders, for example, may not normally interact, and as a result, students may feel intimidated or uncomfortable mixing together in a group in which they are expected to disclose their personal history and feelings in front of each other. Emotional maturity is a major factor in all of this, and it is not always a given that the older students are more mature; in fact, the opposite is often true. We recommend that the group facilitator assess each potential member's emotional maturity and comfort level regarding being part of and sharing feelings in a mixed-grade group.

Reading and Writing Proficiency

The ability of adolescents to express themselves is important during the grieving process. However, not all members are able to express themselves equally well, whether in written or verbal form. The activities (see chapters 7–9) conducted in the CBP 12-week curriculum do incorporate some reading and writing, though they are adaptable to various levels of comfort and skill. The important thing to keep in mind for all facilitators is to assess each adolescent's reading and writing skills and to modify activities as necessary. At the CBP, once we have identified the members who require extra assistance, we often help them individually during the activity while the other members are working. For example, if members struggle with writing, we may have them dictate their responses to us and write them out for them ourselves.

Special Education Status

At the CBP, we believe that adolescents in special education classes are able to join bereavement groups with students in mainstream classes. However, the group facilitator needs to assess each adolescent individually to determine the adolescent's comfort level in being a part of a mutual aid support group as well as the adolescent's ability to think abstractly and be self-reflective. Some students in self-contained classrooms may feel anxious about joining a group that consists of students with whom they do not normally interact; others, on the other hand, may crave such an opportunity. Again, it is the responsibility of the group facilitator to assess the best way to treat each member.

Siblings

We have, at times, led groups in which the members' siblings have also participated in the group. (We even had a group with triplets in it!) It is important that the group facilitator talk with each sibling to make sure each is comfortable being in the same group. As long as each sibling is able to share freely in the group, then it is fine for those particular siblings to be together. However, if siblings feel uncomfortable talking about family or personal experiences in front of each other, then the group facilitator will have to come up with an alternative plan to accommodate the siblings (e.g., placing them in two different groups).

Cultural/Racial Backgrounds

As long as issues of stereotypes and culture are brought to the forefront, then group members' ethnic or racial backgrounds should not be a chief concern. The group facilitator should make it clear to the adolescents that differences within the group indicate that everyone has thoughts and traditions regarding death and dying, regardless of how unique or different they appear to some adolescents. The group facilitator must simply remind members of the importance of being open to learning from one another.

Dialect

Of course, even though group members should speak a common language, it is important for them and the group facilitator to be aware of the nuances of language, especially if some students are bilingual. For example, a student may speak English, but may be unfamiliar with certain dialect, including common idiomatic phrases, such as "I feel blue" or "I feel down," in which the words *blue* and *down* are used to convey sadness.

Religious Backgrounds

At times, we at the CBP have led groups in which the members either practice different religions or practice no religion at all. As with race and culture, the adolescents must be taught to embrace the differences and similarities among them in terms of religion, spirituality, or faith in general. The group facilitator must emphasize that different religions believe different things about death and the afterlife (even the existence of an afterlife); because of these differing viewpoints, it is vital that the group members keep an open mind when listening to others' beliefs.

Bereavement-Specific Characteristics

This section discusses the commonalities and differences that exist among group members with regard to the following factors: type of loss, who died, when the loss occurred, and multiple losses versus a single loss.

Type of Loss

It is not always possible to strike a balance between group members who have suffered losses due to sudden deaths (e.g., homicide, suicide, accidents) and those who have experienced anticipatory losses (e.g., old age, chronic illnesses such as cancer or AIDS). What we have discovered, however, is that the most important factor for everyone in the group is that the experience of the loss itself takes precedence over the specifics of or the reasons for the loss. The group facilitator plays a crucial role in helping group members to identify the common bond that exists between all of them and to recognize the similarities and differences between their individual experiences. For example, for an adolescent who lost a loved one to AIDS, knowing that other members in the group had a similar experience helps to lessen the stigma associated with the disease. In cases in which an adolescent is the only person in the group whose loved one died in a particular manner, he may feel isolated. Therefore, it is helpful if the facilitator can somehow strike a balance so that all members, regardless of how or whom they are grieving, feel a connection to one another.

Who Died

Although facilitators strive for balance, that goal is not always possible to achieve. In our experience, people are quick to assume that some deaths are "worse" than others. However, we feel that it is not necessarily "who" died that carries the most significance, but rather the "relationship" between the adolescent and the loved one who died. This is the point we try to emphasize in the group so that members can share their stories and at the same time share the similarities and differences between their experiences. Yet if all of the group members except for one have lost a parent or a primary caretaker, that sole student may feel isolated or forced to lessen the significance of the death he is grieving because his loss somehow does not "equal" the others' experiences. On the other hand, the majority may feel that the sole member may not understand what most of the group members are going through. These situations are not too common in bereavement groups. However, if they do occur, the facilitator must help the group members to understand the commonalities and differences between them so that no member feels bad or alone. This goal can be achieved by reinforcing the point that each member has joined the group due to a significant loss, and although the details of each loss are unique, similarities are still present.

When the Loss Occurred

The passage of time does have some healing attributes, and it is true that with more recent deaths, feelings may be more intense. We have worked with adolescents who have lost a loved one at a wide range of ages: 1, 5, 10, and as recently as one month prior to the group's beginning. We feel that if group-appropriate adolescents are in need of support and feel ready to join a bereavement group, they should be allowed to join, irrespective of when the loss occurred. However, one difficult factor to take into account is the issue of memories. An adolescent who lost a loved one years ago may not have as many memories as other group members who are grieving more recent losses. Reflecting on memories, both good and bad, is a vital part of the grieving process, and many of our activities at the CBP encourage this. For those members with fewer memories, the group facilitator should take special steps to lend support (e.g., talk with the members before leading memory-focused activities, and encourage them to meet with a relative to discuss and complete the activity).

Multiple Losses versus a Single Loss

This factor usually does not have much of an influence in determining group composition. It is quite common for some adolescents to have suffered multiple losses, especially those living in the inner city. Because of the group's time constraints, it is sometimes difficult for these adolescents to have enough time to share what they want about their different losses, so facilitators and group members should work together to devise a plan to accommodate everyone.

Behavioral Characteristics

This section discusses the commonalities and differences that exist among group members with regard to the following factors: peer relations, individual temperament and personality, and emotional maturity.

Peer Relations

For adolescents in particular, getting along with peers is a central concern. At the CBP, we recommend that the group facilitator talk with all members about any previous group experience they might have had. This conversation allows the group facilitator to understand the group members' preexisting peer interactions and to assess what role they may play in the group. Gathering information about group members' social development and peer relationships is imperative if the facilitator is to understand and properly plan for group dynamics. As with any type of group, scapegoating, subgrouping, and monopolizing are often concerns that require attention by the facilitator.

Individual Temperament and Personality

An adolescent's temperament and personality play a large role in both the grieving process and in group composition. It is always helpful to achieve a balance in the group between quieter members and more extroverted members. Facilitators must keep in mind that adolescents bring to the group their own skills in communicating and interacting with others.

Emotional Maturity

As noted earlier, every group member faces numerous challenges and developmental tasks during adolescence. These tasks help to shape the adolescent's emotional, cognitive, and moral development. We at the CBP have found that bereavement groups are stronger and more successful when the members are able to treat the group seriously by demonstrating emotional maturity. All members must be able to do their part to help make the group content more meaningful and also to help achieve the group's purpose.

DETERMINING THE STRUCTURE OF THE GROUP

When planning a bereavement group, it is essential to think in advance about the logistics of the group, which are known as the structure of the group. The facilitator must determine certain "arrangements" when setting up the group, including where and when the group will be held and how certain agency policies, such as confidentiality, will be determined.

Temporal Factors

The time element will have to be carefully considered, including the length of time that will be allotted to each group, how that time will be determined by the logistics of the group, and how many sessions will be able to be held within the period of time that is available.

Duration of the Entire Group

In our research, we have seen bereavement curriculums that consist of 6-, 8-, 10-, and 12-week sessions. It is our opinion that 6- and 8-week groups are not long enough for group members to be able to achieve both individual and group goals. As mentioned earlier, we use a 12-week session model that incorporates the three different stages of bereavement groups: beginning, middle, and ending. No matter how long a bereavement group lasts, members still often experience feelings of loss when it ends. This is a normal part of the last, or ending, stage. Groups that continue for longer than 12 weeks or those that go on indefinitely may adversely affect the "ending" process.

Length of Each Session

We recommend that, if possible, each session be at least one hour long. But keep in mind that this is only a recommendation. This minimum allotment provides sufficient time for members to discuss and complete activities. A rushed group undermines the process of creating a safe, healing atmosphere.

Frequency of Sessions

At the CBP, our groups meet once a week during the 12-week span. We believe that bimonthly sessions are spaced too far apart and that biweekly sessions occur too frequently.

Time of Day for Sessions

Determining a time that is most amenable to adolescents is vital to ensuring the success of the group. Choosing the best time to meet depends a great deal on the setting in which the bereavement group takes place. Whether in a hospital, church, community-based organization, mental health clinic, or school, host agencies will have to determine which time is optimal for the group members and their families. If the group is to meet in a school, then the group facilitator needs to collaborate with the school to choose a class period that students can miss without causing much interference for all concerned. This decision can be especially difficult to make if group members come from a wide variety of classes. We try not to pull students from major classes, such as English, math, science, or history. Instead, we and school personnel would rather that students miss an elective. No matter which class students miss, a system has to be set up that will enable them to catch up on missed assignments and to make up tests and quizzes.

Space Factors

Space considerations have to do with where the group will meet and the varied characteristics and logistics involving the designated space.

Meeting Place

A confidential or private space that promises minimal distractions is essential for a bereavement group. We suggest that the same space be used each week to minimize disruption to the group's development of norms. It is important to try not to select an area that other people have no choice but to use as an entrance, exit, or walk-through space; the constant distraction is bound to be detrimental to creating a safe haven for the adolescent grievers.

Size of Meeting Place

Although a large space is not necessarily a key to meeting the needs of the group or to ensure its success, facilitators should choose a spot that has enough space to allow for chairs to be arranged in a circle. This circular setup encourages open communication and group bonding. Although it is OK for the group to sit on the floor, members sometimes get too comfortable and tend to lose their concentration. Another potentially negative aspect of having the group members sit on the floor is that some of the adolescents may suffer from physical infirmities, such as bad backs or arthritis, that are aggravated by sitting cross-legged. In some cases, adolescents may find it impossible to assume such a position. If there is a window on the door, the facilitator should try to cover it with paper and hang or tape a Do Not Disturb: Group in Progress sign on the outside of the door. Although facilitators should be aware of the need to move chairs or put up signs, there is no reason they can't give some of the group members the opportunity to perform such tasks. To underscore how much we at the CBP value every adolescent we work with, whenever a member of the group is absent, we leave an empty chair in the circle. That way, the circle remains unbroken, and the group is reminded of the importance of everybody's presence.

Mode of Transportation

Assuming that the adolescent bereavement group is meeting somewhere off school grounds, it is crucial that facilitators and parents or guardians think ahead about a number of things. One important factor they should take into account is the matter of how the group members will be able to get to the agency safely and on time.

Agency Policy Regarding Confidentiality

Every agency should have a confidentiality policy in place before beginning preparations to host a bereavement group. All staff and potential group members and their parents or guardians need to be on the same page regarding what information stays in the group and what information does not. At the CBP, we inform our adolescents and their parents and guardians that all information that is shared in the group remains within the group. The only time we deviate from that policy is when we, as the group facilitators, feel that the disclosure of certain information suggests that group members are in danger of harming themselves or others or are in danger of being harmed by someone else. Our policy is to inform each adolescent during outreach and the intake interview that should information of a potentially harmful nature be disclosed within the group, then we have a responsibility to inform other people who are close to those adolescents—such as parents or guardians or school personnel—so that all of us can work together to devise an appropriate plan of action. We make sure that the adolescents in our bereavement groups know implicitly that we will not disclose any information they share without telling them first. We also make it known before the groups get under way that it is imperative that all group members make a commitment to keep the details of the group confidential.

WHAT TO DO IN THE GROUP: DETERMINING CONTENT

When planning a group, it is important to reflect upon what type of activities and discussion would best allow the group's goals to be achieved. It is helpful to balance our discussions with other modalities, such as art, writing, and other group activities, so that interaction and communication are encouraged between the group members.

The purpose of our curriculum is to use a combination of activities and discussion topics to create a safe forum in which adolescents can begin to explore the effects of a loss on their lives and lend support to each other during this process—an hour at a time, once a week, for 12 weeks. Because the curriculum has its foundations in social group work theory, our activities and discussion topics are developed according to what stage the group is in—beginning, middle, or ending. Our group facilitators also use themselves purposefully by modeling many activities that are done within the group. We believe that this method of sharing grief experiences helps to facilitate the healing process.

It is important to note that our curriculum is intended to be a suggested guide to content—not a rigid requirement. We know that unexpected issues arise that take precedence over "following the curriculum," and, as group facilitators, we encourage other facilitators to use the curriculum the way they believe it best fits the unique needs of the groups they are working with at that particular time. Consequently, depending on the stage that the group is in, the group facilitator should feel free to use this curriculum accordingly—continuing, extending, and even substituting activities as needed.

CONDUCTING PRE-GROUP CONTACT: OUTREACH, SCREENING, AND INTAKE INTERVIEW

Before a group begins, the group facilitator has to develop a system to identify members who are appropriate for the group and then prepare them to be in the group. This process is referred to as the pre-group contact phase and is composed of three different parts: outreach and recruitment, screening of potential group members, and the intake interview.

Classroom Outreach and Recruitment

1. Introduce yourself to the teacher and students in the classroom.

2. Explain that you will be conducting one or more bereavement groups in school for adolescents who have experienced the death of someone close to them. Ask the adolescents to raise their hands if they have, during the course of their lifetimes, experienced the death of a loved one. Comment on what you see from their response.

3. Explain that when someone dies, we often experience many different feelings—sadness, anger, guilt, regret, to name a few. We sometimes have a hard time concentrating in school. We also may feel as if no one understands what we are going through. Sometimes, in fact, we are afraid to bring up our feelings at home because we don't want to upset other family members. We may also feel that our friends do not fully understand what we are going through. These are all reasons that adolescents may want to join a group— to get support from other adolescents who have gone through similar experiences.

4. Cover the following points:

    (a) The group is voluntary: Adolescents must want to join this group and should not feel forced to join (even if the group facilitator, teacher, or parent or guardian believes that the group would be beneficial to certain adolescents). Critical to the adolescents' success are their comfort levels.

(b) The group involves personal sharing and listening to other group members.

(c) Parental or guardian permission is required if adolescents wish to join the group.

(d) The group meets once a week for 12 weeks. Because the group meets in a school, group members will miss one class period per week, and that means that work and tests must be made up. The desire to miss a class is not a valid reason to join the group. Sometimes adolescents will want to join the group because they really just want to get out of a class and avoid work. It is imperative that group facilitators get this point across to each adolescent in a one-on-one session.

Although what goes on in the group is confidential, there are exceptions to this rule. It is strongly suggested that group facilitators ask whether anyone knows what the word *confidential* means. Facilitators must then make sure that the adolescents understand that confidentiality means that whatever is said in the group stays within the group.

Confidentiality is an incredibly important requirement; all group members must know that their feelings are respected and that every member feels safe. There are, however, a few exceptions to this rule, and they have to do with what we call the "confidentiality clause": If group facilitators feel concerned that certain group members may be very sad or depressed and thinking about harming themselves, or if group members are being hurt by others, then the group facilitator must talk to the group members so that together they can plan what steps to take next. That plan will likely involve speaking to someone at the school (a teacher, counselor, or the principal) and at the adolescents' homes (parents or guardians).

The group facilitators should make it clear that they will not take any steps relating to such problems without talking to the adolescents first. This is where the confidentiality clause plays a major role: Although every group member must keep everything 100 percent confidential, the facilitator is required to adhere only to 99 ¾ percent confidentiality. In other words, on some occasions, the facilitator may have to share problems with parents or school officials in order to make sure that everyone in the group remains safe.

If they express interest in joining the group, adolescents should be instructed by facilitators to go see their designated contact person (e.g., principal, guidance counselor, teacher) and sign up. Meanwhile, facilitators should announce that they will come back the following week and speak individually with those adolescents who are interested, and together they will determine whether the group is appropriate for the adolescent. Each adolescent who is interested will receive a permission slip (see Appendix A) that the parent or guardian must sign in order for the adolescent to be permitted to join the group. Once the adolescent brings in the signed Parent/Guardian Permission Slip, the facilitator should explain to the adolescent that the two of them will meet again later for something called an intake interview (see Appendix B), which is a chance for the adolescent to find out more about the group and for the group facilitator to find out more about the adolescent's experiences. The group will not begin until all the intakes have been completed. The intake interview is discussed in detail later in this chapter, in the section titled "Intake Interview: Conducting a Personal History of Loss."

Referrals: Another Method of Recruitment

Another means of recruiting potential group members is via referral. Depending on the host agency, wonderful referral sources can often be found. In schools, for example, principals, teachers, and guidance counselors often have knowledge of students who have experienced a death. No matter the setting, it is helpful to have a meeting with your referral sources and have them brainstorm adolescents whom they believe may benefit from a bereavement group. Encourage them to speak with these adolescents to let them know about the group. The referral source should inform the adolescents that the group facilitator will return to the school or other locale shortly and explain more about the bereavement group in person.

Parental or guardian referrals are another important source of recruitment. Any opportunity to meet with parents or guardians is encouraged; a good way to meet parents and guardians is to attend PTA or orientation meetings. It is important to educate parents and guardians about the potential benefits of their adolescents' participation in a bereavement group and to explore any concerns the parents or guardians may have. Often, parents and guardians appreciate the opportunity for their adolescents to receive support that the adults are unable or not yet in a position to give. On other occasions, parents or guardians may be concerned about their adolescents' participating: Perhaps the details of the death are too personal and the parent or guardian does not wish the adolescent to disclose any information about the circumstances surrounding the death of the loved one; perhaps the parent or guardian is worried that their adolescent will become more upset by being in the group; the parent or guardian may also wonder if the group favors any specific religious or cultural beliefs. All of these reactions are common and can be addressed during an orientation by the group facilitator.

If parents or guardians are worried about their adolescents' sharing personal information in the group, it is important that the group facilitator discuss the confidentiality rule and point out that it is up to each adolescent to choose to share what is comfortable to share. At Interfaith Neighbors, we acknowledge that the guilt and stigma that sometimes accompany certain deaths can often be lessened when adolescents realize they are not alone in feeling responsible and that they are not to be blamed for the death.

If parents and guardians are worried that their adolescents may become more upset by participating in the group, it is important for facilitators to acknowledge that adolescents frequently show their grief by way of their behavior (in school, at home, and with peers) and often feel alone and isolated. Participating in a bereavement group will doubtless bring up feelings of grief because the environment gives adolescents permission to experience and share what they are feeling. Although such disclosures may indeed leave these adolescents feeling sadder before they feel better, the importance of their realizing that they are not alone has many benefits. Parents and guardians should be informed that if the group facilitator becomes concerned about the welfare of a particular adolescent, then the facilitator will let them know that.

The manner in which concerns about religious and cultural beliefs are handled will depend on the host agency's target population and policies. Because Interfaith Neighbors is a secular, nonreligious agency, we inform parents and guardians that it creates an environment in which all religious and spiritual beliefs (and the lack of them) are respected and acknowledged. We are also able to alter certain activities to accommodate different beliefs. For example, we once had an adolescent in one of our groups whose family was uncomfortable with the idea of writing a letter to his loved one because, in his religion, such communication was not allowed. As a result, instead of writing a letter *to* his loved one, he wrote a few words *about* his loved one, and he chose not to release a balloon (which was the culmination of the activity). After the activity, this adolescent explained why he did what he did, talked about his beliefs to the group, and in the process taught his fellow group members something new. Thus he was able to share something unique, teach others, and feel supported—all at the same time.

Screening of Potential Group Members

When we do outreach, we ask any interested adolescents to sign up with their designated contact person. Once these potential group members have been identified, we come back and meet one-on-one with each adolescent and talk about the adolescent's interest in joining a bereavement group as well as his or her particular needs and specific situation. This meeting is intended to help determine who is appropriate and ready to join a bereavement group. This process of assessing an adolescent's suitability for a group is referred to as screening.

Determining who will benefit most from being in the group is a complicated task because no one can ever know for certain how adolescents will fare once they join a group. When facilitators sit down with adolescents one-on-one for the first time, we like to know what motivated the adolescents to find out about the group. Facilitators then ask them to tell a little bit about their particular death experience, including who died, when they died, and how they died. It is vital to assess the significance these deaths have had on the adolescents' lives. Although facilitators do not restrict adolescents from joining bereavement groups on the basis of who died or when, we do believe that the adolescents who want to sign up should feel that the deaths were significant events in their lives.

We then provide an overview of the group and discuss the expectations and commitment required of each group member. Afterward, we ask whether the adolescent has any questions or concerns. This meeting is the opportune time for both the adolescent and the group facilitator to address any concerns about the adolescent's joining the group. For example, the adolescent may not feel ready to share his or her story and may feel anxious about this aspect of the group. This hesitance by the adolescent might indicate to the adolescent and the facilitator that he or she may not be ready to join. In another example, the adolescent may want to join the group because he or she experienced a different type of loss—other than death—such as parents' divorce or the incarceration of one or both parents or guardians. Our groups are intended only for those who experienced the loss of death.

We have also encountered adolescents who wanted to join a bereavement group because they lost a loved one before they themselves were born. We feel that an adolescent in that type of situation is not appropriate to join a group because his or her circumstance is too different from the other group members'.

However, let's say that an adolescent named Jeff does appear to be a good fit for the group. It is important to note his address and phone number as well as his parent's or guardian's name, work number, and language preference on the Group Member Contact Sheet (see Appendix C). Next, you should give Jeff the permission slip that needs to be signed (see Appendix A), an agency and program brochure, and your business card (if you have one), and inform him that you will be calling his parent or guardian later in the week to introduce yourself and the program as well as to discuss their view of Jeff's interest in joining the bereavement group. In general, we have found it helpful to remind the parent or guardian about the permission slip during that phone conversation and also give the adolescent a deadline for returning the permission slip.

Although there are no set rules about what to assess while screening prospective group members, we have found that a few crucial indicators exist to guide you. They are listed as follows:

Emotional/mental state: It is important to gauge the emotional state of every potential group member. The adolescent needs to feel that he or she can commit to the group and be an active member. Adolescents who exhibit severe grief reactions that impede their daily functioning may not be ideal candidates for a bereavement group.

Time frame of the loss: All adolescents differ in terms of when they are ready to join a bereavement group; their readiness often relates to when the loss occurred. Although there are no set rules, we usually do not place adolescents in bereavement groups immediately after they have suffered a loss. Adolescents need to feel ready to take on the challenges of a group and should understand clearly what exactly is expected of them as members.

Willingness to share in the group: All potential group members need to know that sharing their stories and listening to others is an expectation of all group members. Therefore, it is imperative that their willingness to do so be assessed. There will always be quieter and more talkative members, but all members need to participate in the activities and share at levels with which they feel comfortable. If adolescents feel unable to share in the group, it is best that they wait until they feel more comfortable.

Social support network: Adolescents with limited social support networks are good candidates for a bereavement group. The group itself is a form of support and presents a special opportunity for those adolescents without other means of support.

Intake Interview: Conducting a Personal History of Loss

The third component of the pre-group contact phase is the intake interview (see Appendix B), during which facilitators conduct personal histories of loss for all group members. The intake interview occurs after it is determined which adolescents are appropriate to join a bereavement group and after all the adolescents have returned the required permission slip signed by their parent or guardian. The purpose of the intake is to enable adolescents to get to know as much as they can about the program and have their questions answered; the intake also enables group facilitators to get to know the particular loss experiences of the adolescents. Conducting an intake gives the group facilitator the opportunity to identify some of the commonalities and differences between the group members and also helps to determine group composition.

At the CBP, we let the adolescents know that we will be doing an intake with everyone who is interested in the program and that the intake contains a number of questions that will be kept confidential, unless the information indicates that certain adolescents are in danger of being hurt or of hurting themselves. We also let the adolescents know that we will be writing down some of their answers so that we will be better able to remember everything they have said.

The CBP intake interview is adaptable to a range of settings and populations. Group facilitators may find it necessary to add or delete certain questions, depending on the particular needs of their population and their environment.

CHAPTER
4

Responsibilities and Characteristics of Bereavement Group Facilitators

The central responsibility of adolescent bereavement group facilitators is to build a culture of mutual aid within the bereavement group—a place where members help each other to cope. Their effective group leadership, we believe, is part art, part science. While guiding the group through its stages of development, facilitators will draw on science: their knowledge about the process of grief, adolescent development, and social group work. They will also employ a complex set of practice skills. The "art" of the work lies in the personal characteristics and style of all the different facilitators. Their ability to build strong connections between and among members is enhanced by their warmth, empathy, optimism, and use of self. Facilitators' relationships with group members, including how and what they share of their own losses, are of central importance to working with adolescents in grief.

CULTIVATING MUTUAL AID IN BEREAVEMENT GROUPS

Facilitators' expertise does not lie in their personal understanding of loss and death; they are not expected to provide wisdom and advice about loss to the group members. Rather, their expertise lies in their ability to bring together young people who share death and loss in common and to help them evolve into a group in which members help each other to cope with their losses. Helping members to build a safe group culture in which they can share their losses and give and receive help and support is the facilitators' central responsibility. Cultivating mutual aid transcends the purpose of the specific group because it is the central purpose of most groups. As such, mutual aid does not occur spontaneously. Facilitators must enable the development of mutual aid consciously and purposely, always remembering that making no intervention at all also makes a statement.

Skills That Are Critical to the Success of Group Facilitators

The following skills are those that group facilitators need to sharpen if they are to be successful in achieving and refining mutual aid. These skills are important also because they help group members to feel safe and therefore able and willing to take risks as they share themselves with others.

Modeling and Encouraging Positive, Supportive Behavior

From the very first meeting of an adolescent bereavement group, members naturally look to the facilitator to gauge how they can and should behave in this group and in future groups as well. For this reason, it is imperative that group facilitators make it a point to model and encourage positive, supportive behavior that group members are expected to display. For example, if Sari is speaking over another group member, the group facilitator needs to let Sari know that her behavior is impeding the progress of the group by saying, perhaps, "Sari, when you speak over Tony, we cannot hear what he has to say. Let's make sure we give everyone a chance to be heard." By addressing Sari in this way, the group facilitator is modeling the importance of listening to everyone and also reinforcing a valuable group norm: that each group member has the right to be heard. Interventions such as these help the group to appreciate and develop appropriate norms and to familiarize themselves with suitable ways in which to interact with each other.

In another instance, some group members may be behaving in a way that causes other group members to become uncomfortable. Let's say, for example, that the group is having a discussion about funerals. The facilitator looks up and notices that two group members are whispering to each other. What should the facilitator do?

(a) Say nothing because the facilitator doesn't really know what to say?

(b) Let it slide because the two group members are usually well behaved and cause no harm?

(c) Stop whatever the group is doing and address the issue by saying, "Tami, I notice that you and Tom are whispering to each other. When people whisper, it makes other group members feel unsafe and uncomfortable. Let's please remember to respect each other's feelings because we want everyone to feel supported and a part of this group."

The correct answer is (c). Facilitators who answer (a) or (b) are, in effect, agreeing that the two members' whispering is permissible. A few years ago at the CBP, co-worker Brenda Robinson reminded us of the term "Silence sanctions." We have come to live by those two words because, if facilitators ignore disruptive behaviors, then they are essentially giving group members permission to continue those behaviors. On the contrary, by using an intervention and commenting that something is inappropriate or disrespectful, facilitators succeed in discouraging the act, setting limits, and helping to develop suitable norms.

Encouraging Group Members to Connect and Bond with Each Other

Open and honest communication takes place when group members connect and bond with each other. In the first few sessions, communication can be effected by simply ensuring that group members are looking at each other—not just at the group facilitator. If the members are not looking at each other, the group facilitator may wish to make a comment such as "Julio, please don't look just at me; look at all your group members. Everyone in the group needs to hear what you are saying." A comment like this reminds members to connect with each other and also helps them to create a bond with their peers.

Reflecting on What Members Have in Common

At the beginning of all bereavement groups, facilitators need to learn what members have in common. Facilitators need to listen actively, consciously remembering what each member has said. Then, depending on what the facilitators hear, they must quickly ascertain what the members have in common and describe their findings to the group. For example, facilitators might offer comments such as the following: "After listening to everyone's introductions, I get the feeling that many of you really don't know how your loved one died" or "It sounds as though many of you don't feel that you have anyone you can talk with about your loss. Clearly, joining this group was a positive choice for you. Now you are together with people with whom you can share your feelings."

Modifying this strategy a bit, a facilitator may choose to become more specific: "In this group, we have three members who have lost a loved one to a violent, unforeseen act; three who have lost someone to a chronic, long-term illness; and two who have had a loved one commit suicide. Although not everyone's loss came about the same way, each of you has feelings about your loved one's death, and we've assembled this group to talk about those feelings." In this example, the facilitator is searching for a commonality, or a common chord. If the facilitator is successful, the group members will begin to feel less alone and more connected and thereby able to make future connections themselves. Discovering what members have in common is a critical skill for all facilitators to possess because, in the process, they are cultivating mutual aid.

Strengthening Mutual Aid

Much of a facilitator's early interventions involve helping group members to see that they can help and support each other during the process of grieving and that it is important to be able to do that. To help group members understand this point, facilitators need to encourage adolescents to talk with each other, using interventions along the way that strengthen the mutual aid nature of the group. For example, a facilitator might say, "Corey said that he doesn't know how to talk to his siblings about the loss. Mary, you said that you were able to do this. Could you please tell Corey how you did this?" Upon hearing this comment, Mary will feel empowered because she knows she is able to help Corey; at the same time, Corey will feel valued and nurtured because he is going to receive support from Mary—support that she wants to give him.

Monitoring Nonverbal Communication

Group facilitators should also be aware of any nonverbal communication among group members. This means they must constantly be aware of the ways group members are behaving. Are the adolescents' eyes downcast, teary, or distant? Are group members' heads down? Are they rolling their eyes in a mocking fashion or acting disinterested? Group facilitators must take time to notice what is going on with their group members; they must never wear blinders. Ideally, a group facilitator who is talking directly to a group member should also be looking peripherally at all of the group members. Facilitators must practice trying to see from all angles—at least as many angles as humanly possible—and use whatever interventions they deem appropriate for different situations. For example, a facilitator who sees a group member with his head down might say, "Toby, your head is down. Are you trying to tell us something?" Or, a facilitator who sees a child rolling her eyes or looking at someone else in a negative way might stop whatever the group is doing and try an intervention such as this: "Sheila, when you roll your eyes at Clarissa, it makes her and other group members feel unsafe. Remember, the purpose of this group is for us to support each other and to listen to each other and to help each other and ourselves. We cannot do that if we feel that our fellow members aren't respecting us. Is there something you disagree with? Please let us know." When the facilitator makes this comment, Sheila knows her actions are important to the group, and Clarissa knows that she is being supported and protected.

Focusing Group Discussions and Asking Directive Questions

An important skill that all facilitators need is the ability to keep group discussions focused on one topic at a time. Early in a bereavement group, members may be feeling nervous about sharing their stories and therefore choose to talk about the weather or the TV movie of the week. When this occurs, it is the group facilitator's job to get the members back on track. Facilitators can and should mention the resistance that they are witnessing and go ahead and discuss it, but they must not allow it to continue. Their job is to redirect the group's conversations so that they pertain to the topic being discussed by the group at that particular time.

Also, early in a bereavement group, the facilitator will need to ask directive questions that tap into why a particular member wants to be in the group. That being the case, the facilitator might choose to ask, "What do you hope to get out of this group?" This question is important in particular because it gives each member the chance to tell the group his or her reasons for joining the group. All of these directive questions are in actuality simple questions that open the lines of communication and give group members a sense of what each of them wants from the group experience. Their expectations are important for group facilitators to remember, should they need to recall a member's reasons for being in the group.

Specialized Characteristics of Bereavement Group Facilitators

This section summarizes the specialized characteristics of bereavement group facilitators that enable them to carry out their responsibilities, such as modeling supportive behavior, cultivating mutual aid as the group begins to bond early on, and searching for commonalities among group members. Facilitators should encourage group members to connect and bond with each other, maintain their focus, and feel safe in an environment. That environment may at first feel strange, but eventually feels normal as group members share their grieving experiences—many of which they never could have felt safe sharing in any other setting.

Feeling Comfortable while Discussing Death

Death is a topic that is difficult for most people to discuss—regardless of their age. In an adolescent bereavement group setting, it is absolutely vital that the facilitator be able to treat this subject much as any other, with an expertise that ensures a high degree of comfort for the group members. Especially during the beginning stage of a bereavement group, adolescents need their facilitator to speak to the subject with an air of confidence, while at the same time showing a natural ability to be empathic.

Bereavement group facilitators need to feel comfortable discussing death and how certain deaths occurred—even if the stories behind them are sad or horrific—because facilitators are counted on by the adolescents in their groups to listen and to care. A bereavement group facilitator needs to explore all the details surrounding a death—whether the death was natural, sudden, or anticipatory. At the CBP, we believe that the group facilitator should use the actual word *death* when discussing the subject with adolescents. Using expressions such as "passing on" or "passing away" may convey an attempt to avoid the topic by talking "around" it rather than "about" it.

Taking Time to Be Self-Reflective about Prior Death Experiences

For facilitators to be successful when talking about death, they must take the time to reflect upon their own prior death experiences so they can understand others' feelings about death as well. If bereavement group facilitators have not successfully dealt with their own feelings, then they may not be able to help others through their own unique loss experiences. The feelings that rise to the surface while people cope with death are many and varied; they may range from relief to guilt to anger to depression to suicidal ideation—and these comprise just a sampling of the emotions that accompany the loss of a loved one. Another important reason for adolescent bereavement group facilitators to take time to reflect upon their own feelings about their own losses is so they are controlling their feelings rather than allowing their feelings to control them.

Enjoying Working with Adolescents

Adolescents are thought by many to be difficult to work with in either individual or group settings. They can be unruly, noisy, impulsive, insensitive, and hypersensitive. They can also be bright, curious, and engaging. Working with this population requires a special kind of group facilitator who is comfortable, self-confident, and enjoys being in their midst. Understanding adolescents' mood swings and their music preferences, their anger and their pain, takes patience, knowledge, and a strong ego. A successful bereavement group facilitator needs to understand the world of the adolescent and be able and willing to acknowledge the difficulties inherent in being an adolescent in today's society.

Having a Basic Understanding of the Grief Process

Bereavement group facilitators must have a basic understanding of the various grief processes and the feelings that accompany them. They also should be aware that not all adolescents grieve in a chronological order (i.e., in a set arrangement of stages of grief). For a more detailed account of the grief process and related feelings, please review chapter 1.

Being Aware of Wide-Ranging Cultural and Religious Grief Practices

On the face of it, it seems only natural for bereavement group facilitators to be aware of differences among people of different backgrounds, yet somehow these differences—which obviously affect the way adolescents grieve—escape their notice at times. The key point here is that facilitators should not dictate the way adolescents grieve, but rather allow adolescents to grieve in the manner in which they feel comfortable. It is a fact of life that adolescents' religious and cultural upbringing play a major role in how they grieve. Some examples gleaned from our CBP groups bear this out: Many of our adolescents believe that if their loved one is in heaven, then they will be reunited with the deceased upon their own death. Contrarily, some of our adolescents believe that once their loved one has died, the person is gone forever, never to be seen or heard from again. Other adolescents believe in doctrines that maintain that once a person dies, he or she is not to be talked about or memorialized. What we at the CBP have learned is that it is incumbent on bereavement group facilitators to acknowledge that all religions and cultures have different values and beliefs. Consequently, facilitators must fulfill their duties without prejudice or assumption, all the while keeping in mind that there is no right or wrong way to grieve.

Being Strong for the Sake of Group Members

Conducting a bereavement group takes much courage, strength, skill, and dedication. It is not easy to be in a room full of adolescents who are terribly saddened by their losses. It is uncomfortable and disconcerting to hear about the 16-year-old brother who was caught in a crossfire and murdered just outside his apartment or to listen to the tale of the mother who fought a slow, painful, and losing battle with AIDS. Accepting this difficult responsibility, however, is the duty of the bereavement group facilitator, who must accept it unconditionally.

At the CBP, we can't help but notice that grief virtually overwhelms the adolescents with whom we meet. At the same time, we acknowledge that it is our responsibility to help them work through their feelings. It is for their sake that bereavement group facilitators be strong, realistic, encouraging, and supportive. The stories that our adolescents share are tragic and traumatic and make us want to cry—the sadness is so intense and overwhelming. But we believe that bereavement group facilitators should not let our emotions control us. We want to be empathic, but we do not want to send a message that crying or showing one's emotions is wrong. For facilitators to let their emotions get the best of them to the extent that they cannot keep from crying minimizes their effectiveness because it prevents them from appearing strong to the adolescents they are charged with helping. If group members see their group facilitator become emotional and cry while hearing a particular story, they may—as a means of protecting the facilitator—decide to discontinue telling their story. That outcome, however, is the exact opposite of what we are seeking. Our philosophy is that it is paramount for bereavement group facilitators to be the rock of the group, to appear unqualifiably strong as they help their adolescents successfully deal with the realities of their losses. Otherwise, the group members will feel they need to take care of the facilitators rather than vice versa.

Being Knowledgeable about Mutual Aid Group Work Theory

Mutual aid occurs when group members share a common cause by both giving and receiving support throughout the evolution of the group. In our experience at the CBP, we have found that one of the major benefits of our groups is that our adolescents learn to feel that they are not alone with their pain and suffering. They realize that they are in the same boat as others who have lost loved ones, and this realization acts as a gateway to their feelings, showing them how to talk, share, laugh, cry, and just plain "be" (Shulman, 1992).

Acting as a Valuable Resource

Bereavement group facilitators must understand the need to act as a valuable resource. One excellent way to help the adolescents in their groups is to research their community's mental health agencies and hospitals and to become familiar with the services offered at these sites. It is crucial, for example, to know which hospital emergency room has an adolescent psychiatric inpatient ward so an adolescent can be referred quickly to that hospital, if necessary. Knowledge of the community's mental health agencies and hospitals is crucial not only during crises, but also during follow-up.

CHAPTER 5

The Evolving Role of the Facilitator during the Three Stages of the Bereavement Group

All bereavement groups have a life of their own and progress through three different stages of development: the beginning stage, the middle stage, and the ending stage (Kurland, 1982). Each stage incorporates different tasks, outcomes, feelings, and roles for both the facilitator and the group members—in our case, adolescent group members.

Although there is no set time frame in which groups progress from one stage to the next, we have developed our curriculum according to the needs of members at each particular stage. As a general guide, we have broken down our curriculum as follows: (a) beginning stage—Weeks 1–4; (b) middle stage—Weeks 5–8; (c) ending stage—Weeks 9–12.

THE BEGINNING STAGE OF GROUP DEVELOPMENT

The beginning phase of a bereavement group sets the stage for the healing process. During the beginning stage, members may feel anxious about their expectations of the group and may therefore exhibit initial distance from the group. Often there is ambivalence among members regarding their wanting to trust the group, yet fearing rejection and feeling vulnerable (Kurland, 1982). Starting with the first session and continuing through the beginning stage of the group, the facilitator plays a more active role, helping to orient members to the group, to each other, to the facilitator, and to the content of the group (Kurland, 1982). As members look for direction and support, the facilitator must model and provide the structure and safety for positive group norms to develop.

Activities and discussion topics used during the beginning group stage are intended to help the group members get to know one another and to begin to feel comfortable sharing with each other their loss experiences. The activities in the beginning stage call for less intimate sharing because group members are still becoming comfortable with each other and learning to trust the facilitator, the other members, and the group process itself.

Principal Objectives of Facilitators during the Beginning Stage

Many researchers have hailed the significance of the beginning stage of mutual aid support groups because it is the time when group norms are established and the time when group members decide whether the group will be beneficial for them. It is also the time when members begin to connect with one another, feel safe within the group, feel a sense of commitment to the group and its purpose, and begin to trust the group (Malekoff, 1997; Steinberg, 1997). If falls on the shoulders of bereavement group facilitators to make sure these objectives are met. By ensuring a safe environment and instilling positive values and norms, facilitators enable adolescents to grieve and help them to give and receive the emotional support they need.

Creating a Comfortable Environment

One primary objective of facilitators is to help create an environment that puts adolescents at ease and lets them know that they are nestled in safe surroundings. A comfortable climate is necessary because it is conducive to nurturing adolescents and making them feel like equal participants. One setup that we have found workable, simple, and successful is one in which everyone, including the facilitator, sits in a circle. This layout affords facilitators a good look at everyone in the group and puts them on the same level as the adolescents—quite a difference from the normal classroom arrangement that adolescents are so familiar with, in which the adult faces them from the front of the room and presents to them as the teacher rather than as the facilitator, or group worker or helper. This setup should be a relief to many group members because it represents a refreshing change and also indicates to adolescents that they are equally worthy participants in the bereavement group.

In bereavement groups that are held in middle and junior high school classrooms (see chapter 6), facilitators may find it necessary to move desks out of the way. If desks and chairs are constructed in one piece (i.e., as single units), then they can just as easily be arranged in a circle. Regardless of the particulars, the key is to invite adolescents to join facilitators in an environment that is more likely to inspire and stimulate them than to dull their senses and intimidate them.

Exuding Confidence

It is essential that the facilitator exude confidence. From the start, the facilitator needs to conduct a group with optimism and a sense that the group can and will make a difference in the lives of its members. The facilitator holds much of the power in the beginning stage of the group: Members look to their facilitator to see how to act, what to share, and to see what is OK and what is not. They will not want to share their innermost thoughts and feelings with a facilitator who does not appear to know what he or she is doing. Adolescents need to feel that their facilitator can keep them safe and protected.

Taking Notice of Everyone in the Group

As group members file into the meeting room, facilitators should make it a point to notice and speak to each of them and address them by name, if possible. They should welcome each adolescent by saying, "Hello" or "Welcome to the group." Facilitators should also tell the members how glad they are to see them and display a warmth that will alleviate the adolescents' anxiety. This approach should continue throughout the group.

Introducing Group Members and Pointing Out Commonalities

In addition to personally welcoming each group member to the meeting room, the facilitator should make it a point to introduce the members to one another upon their arrival. If there is a lot of down time while waiting for members to enter the room, the facilitator should have those who are present participate in activities such as "Four Things in Common." This is a simple activity in which members are asked to figure out what four things they have in common that are not visible to the naked eye. For example, if two of the adolescents have brown eyes, they could not include that commonality as one of the four. However, if two of them have both visited Puerto Rico at one time or another, that commonality would fit the requirements of the activity. This activity encourages members to communicate with one another in a friendly way and also helps the time pass quickly. The facilitator should make sure to ask the adolescents what four commonalities they found. Although at the CBP we don't use this activity every time we begin a new group, we have found this exercise to be an effective icebreaker that helps enliven the group and minimize awkwardness and anxiety during this initial meeting.

Setting the Ground Rules

During the first session of the bereavement group, it is imperative that the facilitator explain the purpose and goals of the group and what is expected of the members. At this point, the group members should be informed that they—not the facilitator—will be doing almost all the talking during the remainder of the group meetings. The facilitator must make it clear that the major objectives of the group are for the members to get to know each other and be supportive of one another throughout the next 12 weeks. The members should be involved in setting the group's ground rules; this helps to ensure that they have a safe place in which to listen, share, respect everyone in the group, and talk one person at a time.

Being Responsible

Bereavement group facilitators must keep in mind that it is vital that they show up for their group meetings on time and to bring with them all the materials they need for that particular group on that given day. In addition to their curricular material, facilitators should bring at least one box of facial tissues, activity worksheets relevant to that day's meeting, an attendance form, and crisis intervention information. The box of facial tissues should be placed on the floor and within easy reach of the group members.

Calling Group Members When They Are Absent

It is important to let members know that they are missed if they are absent. On the first day, the facilitator should mention to the group that he or she will telephone any adolescent who is not present. Because facilitators see their group members only once a week and have little other contact with them, it is important to let them know that they are indeed missed whenever they are not present for the group. This message helps to build a connection between facilitators and group members.

THE MIDDLE STAGE OF GROUP DEVELOPMENT

The middle stage of the group is often more complex, as members begin to open up and show their true selves (Kurland, 1982). Members may test the group facilitator and each other, in the hopes of determining whether they can trust what is before them. This enables them to use the group to its full potential and enriches the bonds between them. It is during this stage that the facilitator pulls back and allows the group to take more control, while still aiding the development of positive group norms. The facilitator must now help the group to resolve conflict and confront them on behavior that may stray from the group's purpose or mission. This allows members to feel taken care of and to feel safe.

Activities and discussion during the middle stage of group development require more intimate personal sharing, rather than general discussion. By this time, group members have begun to identify what they have in common and what separates their experiences and feelings. Members begin to communicate with each other and rely less on the facilitator for structure. Continued focus is placed on normalizing feelings of grief. The middle weeks also place more emphasis on describing the loved one who died and discussing both positive and negative memories.

Often by the end of the middle stage, members feel more comfortable being in the group. They become aware of what the group means to them and what their contributions are to the group. This new level of comfort often enables members to take more risks and rely less on the facilitator and more on each other. Thus the facilitator can pull back and allow the group to take more control, yet still monitor and evaluate the group's progress. Throughout this stage, the facilitator will continue to validate members' feelings during the group, regulate conflict, and monitor communication patterns (Kurland, 1982).

Principal Objectives of Facilitators during the Middle Stage

As wonderful as the middle stage is, it is also replete with group management issues that need to be addressed as well as conflicts that need to be resolved. In our work at the CBP, we have found that the key to effective interventions is to be direct and to discuss aloud what we are observing in the group. This gives the group the opportunity to voice their opinions and have a say in the matter. During the middle stage, it is extremely important for the group to discuss the issues. As facilitators, we need to be honest and clear, direct and caring. Although most of our bereavement group members are supportive of each other, we do notice instances of nonsupport that require experienced bereavement group facilitation skills.

Helping Members to Relate to Each Other

Sometimes in a group, members may have trouble relating to what others are saying because they have not experienced the same situations. Because of the extensive pre-group interviews they conducted prior to the group's initial meeting, bereavement group facilitators should be able to anticipate such problems. As a result, facilitators should acknowledge what is happening and be able to help the adolescents understand that different people have different experiences with death, and that all of these experiences are normal and OK. As an intervention, for example, a facilitator might say, "Jerry, you may not have experienced the same emotions as Shari when you were told about the death of your loved one, but do you think it is possible for you to put yourself in her position and try to understand what she might be going through? Imagine if, like Shari, you weren't told about the death until one month later: Would you be mad, too?" By helping Jerry relate to Shari's situation, the facilitator is helping Jerry relate to Shari as a human being and thereby cultivating mutual aid.

Urging Members to Listen to Each Other

It is not often difficult for a facilitator to know when bereavement group members are not listening to what others are saying. When adolescents are whispering to someone else when a group member is speaking, the problem is self-evident. In these cases, what we have found to be an excellent intervention is this simple reminder: "Remember, it is important that we listen to each other here so that we can all feel supported." The key is for the facilitator to have the group itself address such conflicts. If this comment by the facilitator fails to get the message across, then chances are good that at issue here is not mere inattentiveness and rudeness, but rather conflict in the group. At this point, the facilitator might try using a less gentle reproof that addresses the conflict directly: "Sam, you and Sarah are being disrespectful by not listening to what others in the group are saying." Although this direct, no-nonsense intervention should be enough to influence Sam and Sarah to change their behavior, it may not serve its purpose. This means that the facilitator must still find some way to understand what is going on in the group—to become aware of the possible causes of the problem—and to try to determine why certain members are not listening to each other. On a positive note, by trying to understand and solve the problem, the facilitator will simultaneously be encouraging most of the group members to explore this conflict that is slowing the group's progress.

Discouraging Disrespect

When a member of the group feels disrespected, it is always best if he or she can discuss the matter with the person who is being disrespectful. However, we know that this is often difficult for adolescents to do. In our groups, we encourage members to talk with each other directly. The facilitator might suggest the following, for example: "Harry, can you tell Cammy how you felt while she was laughing at you?" Such modeling by the facilitator shows group members how to handle disrespectful behavior in the future. After Harry explains how he felt, the facilitator can use this situation to reiterate to the group the purpose of the group by saying, "Remember, the purpose of our group is to create a safe environment in which we can share our thoughts and feelings regarding the death of a loved one. How can we feel safe in here if a member laughs after someone shares?" The facilitator should then listen to the group's responses. Therefore, members will opt for safety and respect rather than cave in and accept the disruptive acting out by other members.

Helping Out When One Member Isn't Sharing Enough

Owing to the mutual aid nature of our 12-week activity-based curriculum, sharing is crucial for all members. Therefore, when a group member does not share, other group members take notice. When this occurs, it may be brought up by group members who feel let down by the quiet member, are frustrated, and feel it necessary to ask the member to do more sharing. One of the members who wants to hear more from the quiet member might go about it diplomatically by commenting, "We know this is hard, but we want to know about you, too." A less patient and more confrontational member might try this approach: "We all talk. Why don't you? It's not fair!" No matter how the request is worded, the quiet member will usually open up and start to share more with the group. The result is that the other group members feel glad that they (or another group member) decided to take it upon themselves and talk about their feelings. Meanwhile, the quiet member is happy that others cared enough to ask and felt that more sharing was important to everybody in the group. As facilitators, we want to reiterate that death is hard to talk about, and some members may need extra encouragement.

Dealing with Members Who Feel They Share Too Much

When a bereavement group member (in this case, Carl) feels as though he has shared too much in a given session, a number of different outcomes can occur. One outcome might be that Carl feels so embarrassed and ashamed that he decides not to return to the group. For a facilitator who anticipates this turn of events, a good idea would be to phone Carl prior to the next meeting, discuss the situation, and work together to rectify the problem so that he will still feel comfortable attending the next meeting. One suggestion that would help Carl—and at the same time ensure that he will come to the next meeting—would be to suggest that he be up-front and honest with the other members and explain that he felt bad and embarrassed that he shared too much at the previous meeting. This gives the group the chance to discuss this situation, and Carl will probably find that most of the other group members will understand his plight and be willing to move on.

Another outcome might be that, during the session in which Carl shares too much, the other group members grow silent, unable to know how exactly to respond. In that instance, the facilitator needs to step in and help the group understand what's going on. One direct intervention that might help would be to look at Carl and say, "Carl, thank you for sharing that information with us. I know that must have been hard for you. Right now, it seems the group doesn't know just how to respond to that comment, but we're listening to you." Trying a different approach, the facilitator might say, "Carl, thank you for sharing that information with us. I am concerned about what you are saying and would like to talk with you further about that at the end of the meeting." By using either of these interventions, the facilitator will succeed in addressing the issue while, at the same time, looking after the interests of both Carl and the group as a whole.

Preventing Problems That Arise When Someone Is Monopolizing

A common problem that occurs in bereavement groups is that one person monopolizes the discussion. We believe it is important to address this issue immediately. If you the facilitator feel that someone is dominating the group discussion, then you must use an intervention that highlights and addresses this situation.

In one intervention, for example, you might say, "Heather seems to have a lot to say during this discussion, but she is not the only one in this group with feelings. Would someone else like to add something to our discussion?" If no one steps up to say anything, you may decide to call on a member for an opinion.

Another intervention you might use would go something like this: "I'd like to hear from more of you about your thoughts and feelings on this topic. Remember that the purpose of this group is for all members to give and get the support they need."

Sometimes the group will have fallen into a routine in which it expects Heather to continue to carry the discussion so that other members won't have to share their own stories. As we have discussed, however, one of your goals as facilitator is to make sure that you provide a safe environment that enables and encourages every member's thoughts and feelings to be discussed and explored.

Appealing to Members Who Feel That the Group Is Not Helpful

Adolescents who feel that the bereavement group is not helpful will usually send a message by failing to attend a meeting one week and then continuing this pattern the following week and then the week after that. Each time you call them at home, they give you a different reason for not having attended or not being able to participate. With repeated absences, you are fairly certain that something is going on in their lives that is affecting their presence in the group. So you discuss the situation with them and ask them questions in the hope that you can learn whether they are having any problems that they are keeping to themselves: "Are you not satisfied?" "Are you not getting what you expected out of the group?" Inevitably, you will find that the group has somehow not been meeting the needs of these members. In their minds, staying away from the group is the only way they know how to tell you that; somehow, making excuses for not showing up is easier than just saying goodbye.

Even if they choose to leave the group during the middle stage, it is important to encourage these members to come back and discuss their feelings with the rest of the group. Perhaps by talking it through with their peers, these adolescents will determine that they do have a real need to belong—a need to get something from others who are grieving the same kinds of losses. Whatever the outcome, it is important for each member as well as the entire group to know that communication between group members is key.

Helping Members Who Are Overwhelmed by Their Emotions

Sometimes adolescents become so overwhelmed by their emotions that they decide to drop out of their bereavement group. Possible explanations they might offer are that (a) the issues are too difficult for them to process or that (b) before the group began meeting, they felt fine, but now they are sad most of the time because they keep thinking about their loved one. As you might expect, it is up to the facilitator and the members to help the group conquer these challenges. By now you know that adolescents often feel worse before they feel better; that is simply part of the grieving process. As the facilitator, it is important that you and the group explore fully these adolescents' reasons for feeling overwhelmed and their desire to quit the group. It might be that some of them were not quite ready to join the bereavement group in the first place. It might even be that some of them need more intensive individual counseling to supplement their group experience. Whatever their reasons, it would benefit both them and the group to talk with their fellow group members about their feelings. They might just discover that other members feel equally overwhelmed but have decided to stick it out. By finding this out, these adolescents cannot help but feel closer and more connected to the others, and consequently feel more a part of the group.

Uplifting Adolescents Who Feel Bad When Others Drop Out of the Group

It is always difficult in a bereavement group when members drop out, whether they do so because they feel overwhelmed or disappointed or because they have encountered a situation beyond their control. For example, some members have dropped out of our CBP groups because they felt they weren't getting what they wanted or needed from the group experience. Others have had to drop out because their families moved to another city or state. Regardless of the reason, the remaining members of the group may end up feeling left behind and abandoned, much as they felt when their loved ones died. These adolescents' feelings of loss are thus reawakened by the departure of other group members. As their facilitator, it is important to acknowledge these feelings and bring them out into the open. One intervention you might try is a statement to the group, such as the following, that meets this problem head-on: "I know that Allan's absence is being felt in this group. I wonder if his departure reminds you of other times in your lives when people have left you." By intentionally using an intervention that addresses the loss of Allan, you will be helping the other group members to acknowledge their sense of loss and understand how to come to grips with it.

THE ENDING STAGE OF GROUP DEVELOPMENT

Adolescents joined the group because they had a need to share their stories of grief and a desire to hear the stories of others. The prospect of leaving the safety and the intimacy of their newfound surroundings is hardly a happy thought. When a bereavement group ends, members often feel yet another loss that leaves them with a profound sense of emptiness. They feel that loss intensely—the loss of support, friendship, safety, and trust. Therefore, the last weeks of the group are structured to allow members to reflect on the group experience and their feelings about having participated. Activities and discussion center on reflecting on their lives and the group experience and on thinking ahead to issues they will face in the future.

By the time the end of the group draws near, members are often quite adept at communicating openly. Discussing how the group has changed and how members have grown are important steps during the ending stage. The fact that the group will soon be ending needs to be addressed by the facilitator and the members, with emphasis placed on successes, regrets, and next steps.

Principal Objectives of Facilitators during the Ending Stage

During the ending stage of the group, the facilitator must help the group members to say goodbye to each other and to help them prepare to leave each other. By this time, group members will have endured their fair share of crying, laughing, and bonding, and many will feel a huge loss. They will feel the loss of support, friendship, safety, and trust. To members, the group represented a place where they could be with others who experienced similar feelings and not feel alone. It is imperative that the facilitator acknowledge these feelings and address them during this stage.

Conversely, group members may also be feeling ready for the group to end, and this, too, should be discussed. Facilitators must tell the members that all these feelings are normal and result from the termination of the group process. Facilitators should make sure to take adequate time to discuss the many triumphs and defeats that the members experienced as well as the goals they realized and the goals they failed to reach. At the very end, facilitators should point out any observable gains that each member made and express confidence in each member's ability to continue to make future gains once the group is over.

Helping Members to Deal with Feelings of Loss All Over Again

During the last few weeks of the ending stage, members will once again begin to acknowledge and experience feelings that they felt they had already worked through during the 12-week curriculum, such as abandonment, sadness, anxiety, worry, and fear. For many group members, reliving these aspects of their group experience can prove unsettling and cause them to feel a loss of control. To help them through this period, facilitators must anticipate that the adolescents will indeed go through this phase and then help them put their feelings in the context of the reality that the group is coming to an end. Facilitators need to identify what is happening to the group members and work to normalize these adolescents' feelings. In the process, they must make sure that the group members know that what they are going through is to be expected during the ending stage of the group and that group members can work through their feelings with the support of their fellow members, the group as an entity, and the facilitator.

Addressing Members' Regression to Earlier Ways of Behaving

Oftentimes during the ending stage of a bereavement group, members return to earlier ways of behaving. They might, for example, return to habits such as giggling or acting nervous or becoming quiet and reserved, even though they have just spent weeks talking and acting the opposite way. Again, for the facilitator, being able to anticipate this behavior and then pointing it out to the group members and reassuring them that this type of behavior is normal will put the adolescents at ease. It is also imperative for the facilitator to point out to everyone what the group members have accomplished during their time together and to help them acknowledge their achievements during the group.

Anticipating Members' Not Showing Up for the Last Few Group Meetings

Skipping the last few group meetings is classic behavior that illustrates how difficult it is to end something that has been so meaningful. Often, group members would rather "leave" than "be left." That being the case, they often find it easiest to say goodbye simply by not showing up for the ending group sessions. It is extremely important that the group facilitator anticipate this behavior. If a group member does not show up for any of the last few sessions, the group facilitator must call the member immediately and help him or her to understand the importance of returning to the group. During the conversation, the facilitator can concede that it is difficult to leave something behind that has been so meaningful and significant, but should at the same time emphasize how important it is to have the opportunity to say goodbye to everyone and to end things on a positive note and with no regrets.

One strategy the facilitator can employ is to talk about how often it is when dealing with death that one can never say things to a loved one. In bereavement groups, however, there is always the chance to say goodbye to group members. The facilitator needs to encourage all group members to talk with one another so they can tell each other goodbye and at the same time discuss how they feel about the group's ending and what they got out of participating in the group for 12 weeks.

Helping Members Who Want the Group to Continue

At the CBP, there has rarely been a group we have facilitated in which one or more group members did not ask us to continue the group. "Why can't this go on all year?" was the question we often heard at the group's ending. Our answer was always the same: "There is never enough time." We would explain that, no matter how long the group was to last, certain members would want it to continue because they found that they were getting so much out of the experience—support, friendship, and a feeling of safety. We believe that our 12-week curriculum is the ideal length of time for a bereavement group because it is by nature a concrete intervention that allows its members to cycle through the various stages of the group as they cycle through their own personal grief journeys. We also believe that 12 weeks is an acceptable amount of time for students to be excused from classes.

Clearing the Air by Confronting Unresolved Doubts and Regrets

The task required of the facilitator when group members begin to have doubts about what they have accomplished during the group is important in that it calls for much discussion and review. It is crucial that the facilitator have the members think back to their group experience and honestly determine what, if any, regrets they have:

> Did the group experience give them what they had hoped for?
>
> Do they have any lingering doubts about their experience?
>
> Do they now have a better grasp of the connection they had—and still have—with their loved one?
>
> Does an opportunity to continue the release of pent-up, painful feelings still exist?
>
> Are they able to look beyond the pain of their loss and think toward the future?
>
> Are they aware of the availability of ongoing support and follow-up services provided by the host agency?

When some members exhibit doubts about what they learned in the group, it is imperative that they talk about them with the entire group so that everyone can hear what those doubts are. It could be, for example, that other members have similar regrets. Other members may have had those same reservations and now feel guilty about not having shared them with the group—perhaps because they were absent too often and therefore unable to provide input. Whatever the doubts or regrets, this is an opportunity for everyone to clear the air.

Staying Focused on Group Members' Needs

It is easy for facilitators to get a bit off course as they near the end of their 12-week bereavement group. After all, even though they must suppress the need to cry when they hear some of the stories shared by the adolescents they are helping, facilitators must also keep from sharing too much of themselves. They need to remind themselves that their job is to help group members help each other—to teach them how to give and receive support. It's one thing for facilitators to touch on their own grief experiences, quite another to go into too much depth. Therefore, although it is imperative that facilitators give of themselves and become personal, they must stay within reasonable boundaries.

Discussing the Need for Follow-Up Services

Discussing the need for follow-up services is an important part of the ending stage because it is true that quite often at the end of a group, bereavement support services are still needed. If some group members wonder how this can be possible, the facilitator needs to point out that the bereavement group represents merely a single step in the grieving process and that—at any given point in the group—all group members are bound to be at different stages of their journey. To be helpful, in a one-on-one setting, the facilitator should have mental health resources available during the ending stage in case there is a need to give out referrals.

GRIEF COUNSELING AND "USE OF SELF"

Along with acknowledging that grief counseling is unique, many in the bereavement field also understand the importance of "use of self" within groups. For example, John Fogarty (1998) says, "Grief counseling is different than counseling of other disorders. Personalization is helpful. Patients quickly realize the true experts in care giving are skilled and also have a history of losses." Susan Cho, Edith Freeman, and Shirley Patterson (1979) report that the use of the vernacular, metaphor, and candor help to establish intimacy when working with adolescents in grief. According to Gary Lloyd (1977), when working with adolescents, a plain comment, such as "It's all right. I've been there," can go a long way to strengthen a working bond.

Furthermore, several humanistic and interpersonal theorists, such as Bugental (1965), Fromm-Reichmann (1959), Jouard (1971), Rogers (1951), Searles (1986), and Sullivan (1953), have also advocated "authenticity, realness, genuineness, and mutuality" in the therapeutic encounter and show an acceptance of the need for therapist self-disclosure generally (Goldstein, 1997).

Our 12-week bereavement curriculum requires that the facilitator model the curriculum, using a personal loss experience. This modeling is often done at the start of the group session as a means of enabling group discussion and communication. It has been our experience that adolescent group members find this helpful to them in that they feel a connection to everyone in the group, including the facilitator. Group members also report that such sharing by the facilitator often shows them that the facilitator understands the grief that they are feeling and is not merely doing a "job."

The key for the facilitator, however, is knowing how much to share and when to share it. Facilitators must be careful not to divulge details of their loss that are too personal. Therefore, we advise group facilitators to share only what they feel is important for the group to know: information that will help these adolescents in their grieving process. Should the members begin asking for further details, it is vital that the facilitator set appropriate boundaries and redirect the conversation. The group forum must never become a place for the facilitator to seek personal support from the group members. Instead, the focus must always remain on the group members and the development of mutual aid.

CHAPTER

6

Bereavement Groups in Schools

To backtrack a bit, in 1994 we at Interfaith Neighbors, Inc., were interested in offering a bereavement group to adolescents who were already receiving services from our agency. We completed the necessary steps outlined in the pre-group planning process (as described in chapter 3) and got the group under way. Thus was born the Children's Bereavement Project (CBP) that we have been discussing in this book. Unfortunately, this initial bereavement group was not well attended. Most of the adolescents who met the group's qualifications lacked the motivation to put in a full day's work at school and then attend a bereavement group that we had scheduled for 5:00 p.m.

Yet, as an agency that believed in our mission, we were not discouraged. We still knew that adolescents in grief have many needs. Therefore, we were still committed to the goal of creating for adolescents in grief a safe environment in which to discuss those needs with others so they would not feel isolated. We became convinced of the merits of hosting bereavement groups in school settings, specifically in junior high and middle schools, and set out to do so. We began meeting with school personnel in East Harlem and Yorkville (our target areas of Manhattan) to get a feel for whether they thought bereavement counseling would be beneficial in their environment. Their answer was an overwhelming and unequivocal yes. All of the school personnel we talked with told us that early and violent death was pervasive in the families and lives of their students. They went on to say that the majority of grieving students were failing subjects, acting out, isolating themselves, and needed much more help than they were currently being offered. Anything that we could provide, they said, would be a big help.

Next, we talked with the adolescents and their parents and guardians about the idea of the adolescents' taking part in bereavement groups during the day at school. Everyone we asked felt it was a good idea to offer students a bereavement group during school hours. They believed that (a) being in a group would help students to become more focused and give them a safe place to talk with other students who had been in the same situation; (b) there would be a reduction in the attrition rate because the adolescents would already be present at the school; and (c) most important, these in-school groups would help students to feel less isolated from their peers and more a part of the mainstream—that the groups would normalize the experience of grief for them.

BENEFITS OF SCHOOL-BASED BEREAVEMENT GROUPS

School-based bereavement groups are beneficial in many ways. The first and most obvious benefit is that group facilitators are physically present in the environment in which adolescents spend the majority of their days. Facilitators are in the unique position of being able to observe behavior, discuss the behavior of group members with school staff, and work collaboratively to help adolescents through major life-changing events. Other benefits exist, and they will be discussed in this section.

Finding a Contact Person to Help Identify and Recruit Group Members

By operating in partnership with schools, bereavement group facilitators are able to work closely with school personnel to identify and recruit prospective group members. While recruiting group members in schools, it is extremely helpful to work with a contact person (preferably a guidance counselor) who knows the students and their different needs. For example, if a guidance counselor has been seeing a student due to acting-out behavior or classroom absences and the student has recently suffered a loss, then that adolescent can and should be referred to the bereavement group. The school-based support staff can keep up-to-date lists of referrals and give them to the group facilitators when they visit the school to begin the outreach and recruitment process.

Working as a Team with the School

How many times have bereavement group facilitators wanted to know more about a student's academic performance, social skills, or behavior in school? How about what the adolescent's family life is like or what issues and concerns the adolescent is dealing with? School personnel offer a wealth of insight into students and their families. Working in a school provides a perfect opportunity for facilitators to work as a team with teachers, the principal, and the facilitators' contact person to fully understand the adolescent.

Working as a team also helps with follow-up and follow-through. If group facilitators need more information about certain students or want to know how these students are performing in the classroom, then they can ask the contact person for more information. Oftentimes, if a student in the group is actively suicidal, the contact person can work with the group facilitator to talk with the family, and together the two can make a referral to a psychiatric emergency room, if they feel that is necessary. Or, for example, if students indicate they are having trouble with certain peers or teachers in the school, the group facilitator can determine if this particular problem is something the contact person should know about in order to help these troubled adolescents the best way possible. Working closely with the contact person is essential in the facilitator's work with school bereavement groups.

Observing Peer Interactions Outside the Group

Within the school setting there are many opportunities for facilitators to observe peer interactions outside the bereavement group. Group facilitators can observe students during lunchtime and classroom breaks to see how group members interact with peers—whether they isolate themselves, draw negative attention to themselves, or are a positive force in the school community. Facilitators can then discuss these observations with their contact person and make an informed decision about how to process this information gathered about students in one-on-one or group settings.

Addressing Adolescents' Academic Needs and Classroom Behavior

Working in the schools provides facilitators with the opportunity to talk with teachers to address students' academic needs and classroom behavior. If a student is having a difficult time in the classroom, facilitators will have a better chance to find out about it and, as previously noted, can discuss the struggles either in the group setting or with the student on a one-to-one basis. Facilitators can also choose to discuss the adolescent's struggles with the adolescent, his or her family, and the teacher.

Normalizing the Experience of Death for Adolescents

Holding bereavement groups in schools normalizes the experience of death for adolescents. It shows them that death is not a taboo subject that is best left swept under the rug. It also helps them to realize that by taking that first important step to join a bereavement group, they are on the road to helping themselves now and in the future. In addition, adolescents learn that bereavement groups serve as stepping-stones for them to reenter the mainstream. After participating in bereavement groups, students typically report that they feel less isolated and more a part of their peer group and school community.

Enriching Schools' Attitudes about Death and Their Approach to Dealing with the Topic

By working in schools, facilitators are in the unique position of being able to enrich the ways students and school personnel approach death and their methods of dealing with this serious and delicate topic. In our capacity as bereavement group facilitators, we sometimes find ourselves acting as consultants when a beloved teacher or student dies. On those occasions, we are called upon to create schoolwide memorial celebrations, set up classroom grieving centers, design memorial walls, and develop and administer specific bereavement curriculum with designated populations. At times we have been asked to facilitate support groups to help teachers express their thoughts and feelings when a colleague has died and to facilitate short-term crisis intervention groups for students, when necessary. For example, after the cataclysmic events of September 11, 2001, we were welcomed into the classrooms of a number of schools in New York City, whereupon we set up separate crisis counseling rooms for teachers and students. Because bereavement group facilitators are familiar with school personnel and vice versa, our presence was considered a comfort, not an intrusion or an annoyance. We believe that death should not be discussed quietly in back rooms; rather, it should be discussed as an important aspect of life and illuminated so people can see it for the universal experience that it is. It is up to us, as bereavement group facilitators, to teach school personnel and students about the stigma that is unfortunately attached to death.

Functioning as Valuable Referral Resources

Working in schools gives bereavement group facilitators the opportunity to function as valuable referral resources for school personnel and parents alike. As social workers involved in a community-based organization, we know most of the referral agencies in our communities or are capable of locating them. This special talent comes in handy when we are working with families who are grieving the loss of a loved one because it enables us to make referrals for adolescents, siblings, parents, or the family as a whole, and at the same time it brings us closer to everyone involved in the grieving process. As a result, parents and guardians, adolescents, and school personnel feel that they can depend on us because they view us not only as precious allies, but also as capable, valuable resources intent on helping them with their grieving adolescents.

SERVICE DELIVERY STEPS

In order to begin working in any school setting, bereavement group facilitators will need to follow the instructions outlined in this section. Service Delivery Steps are described in detail and appear in checklist form as Appendix D.

Initiating Your Relationship with the School

Your first step is to send an informational letter to the school principal (see Appendix E) on agency letterhead. In the letter, you should introduce and describe your agency and explain the bereavement program. You should also inform the principal that you would like to arrange a meeting in the near future to talk about the bereavement program and the possibility of scheduling classroom outreach. Make sure to close the letter by suggesting that the two of you meet in person. Tell the principal that you will call back soon to personally discuss the bereavement program. If you have brochures available that provide additional detailed information about your agency or your bereavement program, you should be sure to enclose them with this letter.

Unless you hear from the principal right away, follow through on your promise to get back in touch shortly. If the principal gets back to you soon, shows an interest in the program, and would like to meet with you, schedule a mutually convenient time for the two of you to meet. Bring to the meeting all the materials that explain your agency or program as well as samples of the forms and memos you use during the course of the bereavement group: agency and program brochures and newsletters; an overview of the bereavement group curriculum (see Appendix F); a copy of the school personnel memo (see Appendix G), which explains the bereavement program; and the parent/guardian permission slip, which you will later copy onto school letterhead (see Appendix A).

During your meeting with the principal, discuss the framework of your agency or group and all of the important details associated with it. By doing so, you will be providing the principal with enough information to ensure proper implementation of the program in the school.

Selecting a Contact Person

The principal will first need to select a contact person for you. The contact person will be your most important link to the school—the person you will talk and stay in touch with about the program, the outreach, and the schedule. A good option is a guidance professional, but in cases in which a school does not have a guidance department, any school professional who knows the students and the intricacies of the school schedule will be able to fill that role adequately. This contact person will help you through the maze of classroom schedule changes, field trip excursions, half days, and other unexpected or special events. Regardless of who the contact person is, he or she must be someone who keeps abreast of the goings-on at the school and is always available to you when you need assistance. If you don't have a contact person, you will lose valuable time due to unexpected events that take place during scheduled groups.

Determining When the Group Will Meet

The principal will probably work closely with the contact person at the beginning, carefully checking the school schedule to determine which period will serve as the ideal time for the bereavement group to meet. At the CBP, we generally prefer that our group meets during elective periods so that students will not miss a major subject. In a perfect world, it should work this way, but of course sometimes it does not. In a group of eight, there might be one student who has to miss a major subject, whereas the others don't. It really depends on the school and the students' class schedules.

On a positive note, most families believe that the bereavement group is important enough to warrant missing an academic subject, so you will probably discover that there is a very low attrition rate in your school-based meetings. If we at the CBP happen to lose students because of a conflict with academics, we try to offer individual counseling so that these adolescents will receive attention and guidance. You may wonder why we do not choose to offer this group during lunchtime. The answer is simple: No one will attend. Lunchtime is the one free period most students have during the day, and experience tells us that they would rather not miss it.

Choosing the Ideal Location for the Group

In addition to choosing a permanent time for conducting your bereavement group, it is important to secure a consistent and confidential place to conduct the initial meeting, the intakes, and the group itself. When you meet with one student, perhaps an empty classroom or small office will suffice. When the entire group meets, you will need much more room—enough to accommodate you and the 8 to 10 students in your group.

Obtaining a Copy of the Official School Rules

Before getting started, you will need to obtain a list of the official school rules as well as a copy of the school's parent's manual, which includes a statement describing the school's philosophy. This information enables facilitators to stay on the same page as the school's officials. For example, if it is school policy that students are not allowed to leave the school building during the school day without parental permission, group facilitators need to make sure they get an OK from parents and school personnel before taking the group outside. Facilitators may therefore be required to use special permission slips on these occasions.

Having a School Calendar on Hand

It is always helpful to have a copy of the school calendar on hand before beginning your group meetings. This calendar will help you in a number of ways as you plan your group's activities. Most important, it will provide you with a handy way of keeping up with various school activities, trips, and vacations.

Developing a Crisis Intervention Plan

It is inevitable that there will be certain meetings during which student crises will occur. That's why it is imperative to establish a plan of action in the event that a student needs to be taken to the psychiatric emergency room.

It is important to know beforehand who needs to be informed of a crisis: The principal? Your contact person? The parent or guardian? Once you let them know about the situation, where will you go from there?

In addition, facilitators need to know beforehand how the concept of confidentiality works in the school. We at the CBP tell school officials that we will let them know if we are concerned about a child's physical or emotional safety; otherwise, we will maintain confidentiality with regard to everything said in the group. Keep in mind, though, that principals need to agree with our decision if we are to be able to facilitate bereavement groups in their schools.

Arranging Correspondence with the School

The group facilitator must make sure that there is a way to correspond with the school and vice versa. For example, if a teacher needs to leave you a message concerning a student, is there a place where you will be able to find it? Perhaps a bulletin board or a mailbox in the main office will serve that purpose.

Summarizing the Bereavement Group Curriculum

Facilitators should provide an overview of the 12-week curriculum to the appropriate school officials (see Appendix F). In the process, they should give the principal and the contact person the proposed bereavement group schedule, including the dates of the balloon-release event and the Celebration of Life event.

Initiating Your Relationship with the Adolescents

Well before the bereavement group gets started, facilitators and school officials have many questions to ponder: When will the outreach be done? Who will introduce the facilitator to the students? Where will the facilitator do the outreach? Which students will the facilitator be targeting? These are all important questions the facilitator needs to discuss with the principal and the contact person regarding outreach to attract group-appropriate adolescents.

Deciding on Outreach Procedures

In our experience at the CBP, we have found that the best way to do outreach is by going "classroom to classroom," as we are accustomed to referring to it; but we have also performed outreach in auditoriums, homerooms, advisory rooms, gym classes, lunchrooms, and the like. The worst place that we have done outreach has been outside the school building, during recess. If this is the only opportunity you have to do outreach, try your hardest to change the time of your outreach. During recess or simply outside in the open air, students are distracted and unable to sit still long enough to listen to the information you are disseminating.

Prior to outreach, make sure to meet with all the school personnel to discuss the details of the outreach procedures that have been agreed upon. This meeting should ideally include the principal, the contact person, the teacher, and the bereavement group facilitator, so it is important that all four find a time that is mutually convenient.

This meeting is crucial to the success of the program. By listening to an explanation of the program in full detail, teachers will learn and appreciate what is going on. This meeting will help them to understand the importance of the bereavement group program and also let them know how the project's outreach and intake procedures might affect them and their classroom teaching time. Teachers are very protective of their teaching time, so it is important that they be made aware that certain students may be pulled from their classes to attend various interviews by the CBP staff. What follows is the simplified version of the three-step outreach plan we use:

1. *The classroom outreach*

   The group facilitator will need to visit the individual classrooms to talk with students about the bereavement support group. This classroom presentation should take no longer than 5 to 8 minutes per class. After the presentation, students are instructed to see their designated contact person that day to sign up, if they wish. (See chapter 3, which discusses pre-group planning, for a more thorough description of conducting outreach.)

2. ***The pre-group screening interview***

   The first time they get together one-on-one, the student and the group facilitator will meet for 15 minutes. The purposes of this meeting are (a) to introduce the bereavement facilitator to the student, (b) to give the facilitator a chance to understand why the student wants to participate in the bereavement group, and (c) to decide if the adolescent is group appropriate. (For more information, see chapter 3.) During this initial meeting, the student will be given the school permission slip, which must be signed by a parent or guardian before the intake can be done. The group facilitator will also fill out the Group Member Contact Sheet (Appendix C), which includes the adolescent's relevant contact information.

3. ***The intake interview***

   The purpose of the second one-on-one meeting between the student and the group facilitator will be to complete the intake interview, or intake/assessment. This step generally takes about 30 minutes. The interview consists of questions concerning family history, the history of the death, coping mechanisms, the funeral, religious beliefs, and the student's perception of safety and violence (see Appendix B).

Copying the Permission Slips onto School Letterhead

During your conversations with parents and guardians, it is essential that you discuss the Parent/Guardian Permission Slip (Appendix A) and explain the significance of the principal's signature on the form. All facilitators need to explain that the principal's signature ensures that the school and the bereavement group are working in collaboration and that the school is 100 percent behind the efforts of the bereavement group. To highlight the official nature of the agreement, you should photocopy the Parent/Guardian Permission Slip onto the school's letterhead and then hand it out to prospective group members during the intake interview.

Getting the Permission Slips Signed

Judging by our experience at the CBP, we have found that what works best is to call the parents or guardians *the same night* of the initial meeting with their children to introduce yourself as the bereavement group facilitator. A good idea is to ask the parents or guardians whether their child has mentioned the group. If their answer is yes, ask if they have any questions they would like to ask you. If their answer is no, explain the nature of the group as well as its purpose and what is expected of the children. Make sure that the parents or guardians feel at ease and are comfortable knowing that they can, whenever they feel it necessary, contact you at any time during the 12-week group session. If the parents or guardians feel that their child will benefit from joining, remind them to sign the permission slip. Next, ask to speak with the adolescent, and explain exactly where and to whom to return the permission slip the next day.

Preparing to Facilitate Your First Bereavement Group

It is always best to have your contact person call you, or for you to call the contact person, when the permission slips have been returned. Next, arrange a time to come to the school to conduct individual intake interviews with group members who have had their permission slips signed. It is helpful if your contact person can check the school roster to see if the students whose permission slips have been signed are, in fact, in school the day you plan to visit. If you forget to ask the contact person and simply take your chances that the students will be in school on the day you show up, you will soon learn how problematic this misstep can be. The process becomes frustrating when you travel to the school and find that the children are unavailable. (They may be absent, in the middle of taking a test, meeting with a teacher or the principal, or otherwise unavailable.) Clearly it's well worth the time to do as much pre-interview planning as you possibly can with your contact person.

Now you are ready to begin facilitating your first bereavement group. But first, congratulate yourself. You did it!

MANAGING EVERYDAY OCCURRENCES AT THE SCHOOL

As outlined thus far, there are many advantages to working within a school setting. Still, it is not a simple task. Contact people can be difficult to track down. Crises occur and principals are called out of the building. Fire alarms go off right as you enter. Field trips take place without your knowledge—regardless of how prepared you are. Statewide testing is going on during your group period. Because of these unknowns, it is important that agencies begin their work with schools knowing full well what might happen on any given day. Although the unexpected does occur, it doesn't have to keep you running through a maze.

Taking the School's Pulse

Schools can be extremely difficult to become accustomed to when you are not part of the everyday drama. Especially when you are working for an outside agency, you must be prepared to be flexible; due to the hectic nature of the average school day, very few windows of opportunity are open to you. The more accommodating your agency can be, the better off your relationship will be with the school. Principals are busy, teachers are harried, and everyone has his or her own agenda. While working for the CBP, we have often gone to schools for meetings, only to learn that the principal has been called out of the office for the day to attend a special conference or districtwide meeting. Rather than get angry or feel personally affronted, it is important that you understand the nature of the system you are working within. It is extremely important for the group facilitator to be patient and understanding throughout this process.

Learning the Art of Nurturing Your Relationship with School Officials

There is an art to collaborating with a school that takes time, patience, and the building of relationships with those who work for the school. We have found, for example, that if we drop updates about group members into certain teachers' mailboxes, these teachers will feel more a part of the group experience. During the holiday season, we will distribute sweet treats to the school office, accompanied by a card that reads, "Happy holidays from the Children's Bereavement Project." We touch base with the principal and the referral source regularly and ask for any and all feedback on how we are doing. Most important, we are truly nondefensive, open to criticism—both positive and negative— and happy and willing to make whatever changes we deem necessary and appropriate. By consistently staying in contact with school personnel, we are at the same time nurturing our evolving relationship. This approach is extremely helpful for agencies that plan to return to the school the following year to run bereavement groups once again. If you are pleasant, effective, and flexible, then principals, teachers, contact people, and office staff will remember you and look forward to having you back the next year. By always being considerate and taking the time now to cultivate your relationship with the school, your work the following year will be cut in half. The school's employees will know you, like you, and want to help you.

Building a Solid Relationship with Office Staff

It is both helpful and essential to get to know the office staff in the school where you will be working. In our many years of experience conducting bereavement groups in schools, we have found that the office personnel are the individuals with whom you will actually communicate the most. They are the ones who always know whether a field trip is taking place, whether a citywide test is being given, which students are absent on any given day, and which specific classes are affected by the goings-on. Office staff are invaluable to the smooth operation of the school and to your bereavement group.

Once you build a solid relationship with these indispensable school employees and explain your group program to them, you will find that most of them become your biggest supporters. They will look forward to your visits and root for your group to be successful.

One thing you can depend on is that the office staff will always be available to help you. After all, they are the ones who answer the phone, know the families of students, and are able to get you whatever materials you need in a timely fashion. They also know where teachers can be located when classes unexpectedly meet in different rooms and which teachers are being substituted for on any given day. Suffice it to say, your relationship with the office staff is priceless. If any unusual or extraordinary situations should arise—situations that you absolutely must know about—the chances are excellent that the office staff will be both willing and able to help you.

Keeping School Employees Apprised of Your Group's Composition

Another important reminder is that once you have formed your bereavement group, you need to write a memo to the principal, your contact person, and all school personnel, informing them that you have decided on the composition of your group and letting them know the names of all the students who comprise it. By writing this memo, not only will you be indicating that you wish to maintain an ongoing relationship with the school's employees, but you will also be showing them that you respect them. As underscored previously, teachers generally dislike it when their students are taken out of their class to attend counseling groups, but if they are aware of what exactly is going on and who is receiving what service and when, they are much more likely to support both you and your project.

Calling in Advance

One of the most important lessons we have learned in our work with schools is to call first before you leave your office or your home to attend a school or group meeting. Although you cannot always have a 100 percent guarantee that your school or bereavement group meeting will in fact take place, picking up the telephone and calling the school will definitely give you a much better chance of success.

We cannot stress this point enough: Last-minute changes frequently occur in schools. What we have found is that it never hurts to place this phone call, and it always helps. To illustrate the importance of thinking ahead, in the past we have gone to schools without phoning in advance, only to discover that a bomb threat had been called in and the school had been evacuated, or that a fire had erupted on the first floor and the students' classes had been forced to be moved to the school next door.

Notifying Your Contact Person Whenever Members Are Absent

For a couple of reasons, it is always best to notify your contact person whenever a student in your bereavement group is absent from a meeting. First, by reporting the absence, you are helping the school keep tabs on its students. Second, if a group member fails to show up for the meeting but was present during the school day or vice versa, then you know that something went awry. When you report the absence, it allows the group facilitator, the principal, the contact person, and the adolescent to work together to address the issue and resolve any problems that this absence already has caused or may cause in the future.

Meeting in Your Bereavement Group for the First Time

On the first day of your bereavement group, have the students meet you in the main school office at the designated starting time for the group meeting. This way, everyone in the group can walk to the meeting place together, as one, to give everyone a feeling of harmony. Judging by our experience at the CBP, we know that this method of meeting as a group for the first time eliminates much potential confusion. Once you show the members exactly where the group will be meeting in the future, they will find it easier to get there on their own.

Preparing a Student Room Schedule

This schedule, prepared in advance of the group's inaugural meeting, lets you know which class your group members are supposed to be in during the group meeting. This information can be a big help to you because there's always the chance one or more members will get lost or forget to come. If you know where in the school the group members should be, you won't have to worry about chasing them down. If you think they have possibly forgotten about the meeting or have become confused about the location, you can simply place a phone call to the classroom where they should be at that time (see Appendix H).

Reaching Out to Parents: Why It Is Crucial

Reaching out to parents is the most important, yet possibly the most diffi-cult, aspect of your work as a bereavement group facilitator in a school. As strange as it may seem, students do not always know their own home phone number. So, when you call a student's home on the evening before the initial meeting, it is surprising and rather disconcerting to find that you have reached the wrong number or a disconnected line. Another problem that arises from time to time is that many students simply do not have home phones, or their parents or guardians do not work. If the latter is true, then you have no way of reaching either the students or their parents or guardians. Although it is true that writing letters is one way to eliminate this problem, keep in mind that it takes a very conscientious parent or guardian to follow through and call you back after receiving a letter. To magnify the problem, this form of communication uses up a lot more time, depending on the mail delivery system in your community.

At the CBP, we have found that working with the school personnel helps us to get the information we need—and a lot more quickly. When we are concerned about a family, we talk with the school staff. They have always been most helpful when it comes to providing us with correct contact names and, when available, correct phone numbers. As a bonus, these school employees have been happy to give us feedback on the level of involvement the family has previously shown when dealing with school-related matters. In the past, when we have asked for it, school staff have even arranged meetings between us and the families in question.

The staff of the CBP truly believe that all parents are interested in what their children are doing in school. Furthermore, we believe that the more persistent we are in involving entire families in their adolescents' activities, the more involved the families will want to become. As a result, we doggedly try to help parents and guardians understand that bereavement groups are an integral part of their children's school life. We also want parents and guardians to know that we are available to them if they have any questions or concerns. As a matter of fact, parents often do call us during the course of our bereavement groups to ask questions about their children, to tell us how they feel about their children's progress (e.g., whether their children have begun to open up), or to get referrals for their other children or for themselves. We believe that one of the primary reasons parents and guardians respond positively to us is that we make ourselves available. One reason we seem approachable to families is that we make it a habit to phone each family periodically throughout the course of each 12-week session. Keeping confidentiality guidelines in mind, we discuss the bereavement group and how their child is doing in the group, and we also ask them for their feedback and whether they have any questions or concerns.

PART

CHAPTER
7
Activities for the Beginning Stage

Like the middle and ending stages of any adolescent bereavement group, the beginning stage has a life uniquely its own (Kurland, 1982). Here, at the outset of Part II of this book, chapter 7 showcases the distinct characteristics of the beginning stage, including the different feelings, roles, tasks, and outcomes intrinsic to both the group facilitator and the group members. Although the activities presented here in Part II serve as a blueprint for other agencies to use as a guide for setting up and running their own adolescent bereavement groups, for purposes of convenience, we are presenting them as though they are taking place in a middle or junior high school.

NECESSARY PREPARATIONS FOR STARTING YOUR GROUP SESSIONS

The beginning stage of an adolescent bereavement group lays the groundwork for the healing process for adolescents who are grieving the loss of a loved one. It also requires certain preparations. Once all the pre-group planning has been completed, the group can begin. As group facilitator, you should keep in mind that certain aspects and requirements of the beginning stage will inevitably and naturally carry over into the middle and ending stages as well. For example, in Week 1, under the category "Materials," you will be instructed to provide facial tissues to your group members. Yet you will also need to provide facial tissues during every session—all the way through Week 12. The point is, as you become more comfortable throughout the 12-week curriculum, you will find it necessary yet simple and natural to meet a number of requirements and apply normal procedural steps as you adapt the curriculum to satisfy the unique needs of your particular group.

Another essential preparatory step you will need to take prior to Week 1 is to obtain folders with inside pockets—one for each group member. As you progress through the group, be sure to collect group members' original activities for each week and place them in the folders. These folders will eventually be given to each group member during Week 11. On the outside of each folder, you will need to write each group member's name with a crayon or colored pencil. On the inside left of each folder you can affix your business card either by stapling or taping it to the folder or using a paper clip; then, inside the left-hand pocket, you should insert any other relevant follow-up or referral information provided by your host agency. In the right-hand pocket, you will be able to store—in chronological order from front to back—the adolescent's original works (poems, letters, completed activities, etc.). Remember that these folders will be given to group members during Week 11: Folders and Termination **(see page 159).**

The first session of the group is important also because it provides group members with their first glimpse of the bereavement group environment. These adolescents should leave the first session having had the opportunity to begin to get to know each other and learn about each other's feelings about joining the group. This experience allows them to see both what they have in common and what they don't have in common with others in the group and, regardless of their similarities and differences, to feel connected to one another and the group's purpose.

You should plan to arrive at the group's meeting site before the members, so you will have ample time to arrange the chairs in a circle. A major advantage of this setup is that it prevents any physical barriers from interrupting the flow of ideas from member to member, thus amplifying communication. When—for whatever reason—members are absent, their chairs are still placed in the circle; this signifies that their presence is missed and that the group still remembers and values them. Keep in mind that chairs alone, rather than chairs and tables, are preferred for seating adolescents; otherwise, some group members who are tired may have a tendency to lay their heads on the tables. If this setup is difficult or impossible to arrange, do the best you can to compensate. Make sure the box of facial tissues is placed in an accessible spot, such as on the floor in the center of the circle. By placing it there, you are reminding adolescents that it's OK if they cry.

One rule that you need to make clear—preferably during your pre-group interviews with the adolescents—is that it is absolutely necessary for the group to start and end on time each week. First, we want members to know that they are expected to be responsible to themselves and to the group as a whole. Second, we want members to keep in mind that there is a time limit per session. Therefore, if they wish to bring up something at the meeting, they should not wait until the end, as they may not have the opportunity to discuss their concern. In our CBP bereavement groups, as an aid to adolescents who may find it crucial to discuss a topic, we let them know when there are only 10 minutes remaining in the session. We find that this helps ensure that no adolescent leaves the group without having the opportunity to discuss something of importance. Often, a member will bring up something just as the bell rings. When this happens, we make sure to check with the adolescent after the group has finished, and then we encourage the individual to bring up the topic at the next meeting. Owing to the nature of certain activities, some will occasionally spill over to the next session the following week. This is normal, but you don't want to run continuously behind schedule and fall into the habit of playing catch-up. Therefore, it is wise to keep an eye on the clock and try to fit each activity into the allotted time slot that has been set aside for it.

YOUR ROLE IN PROMOTING POSITIVE GROUP NORMS

Starting with the first session and continuing throughout the beginning stage, you, as facilitator of the bereavement group, will play an increasingly active role. You will need to help orient members to the group as a whole, to each other as individuals, to you as their facilitator, and to the content of the group (Kurland, 1982). As members continue to seek direction and support, you must help them by modeling proper behavior and appropriate use of self, and providing these adolescents with the structure and safety that put their minds at ease and enable positive group norms to develop.

Positive group norms refer to all aspects of a group that make it a safe haven. Included among the various behaviors that make a group safe are the following: showing respect; communicating honestly; sharing in a safe, confidential manner; building trust; and taking positive risks. All groups set certain rules and expectations regarding issues such as attendance, behavior, and confidentiality. Yet, whereas rules are intended to affect behavior, norms constitute the actual behavior that eventually is established and that comes to be expected. If a rule is stated but not followed, then the unhealthy behavior that follows as a consequence becomes the norm within the group. Therefore, in order to achieve the desired group norms, any negative behavior or unhealthy communication patterns (whether verbal or nonverbal) must be addressed by you and the group at the precise moment that they occur. By recognizing and halting undesirable behavior on the spot (i.e., exactly when it occurs), you are modeling desirable behavior and at the same time showing the adolescents in your group that you care about them and will work to make the group safe. By ignoring undesirable behavior and permitting it to continue, you are sending the opposite message and are in effect showing adolescents in your group that they cannot trust the group process. As a consequence, the group will be undermined. (For more on this topic in Part I, see chapter 4.)

INTRODUCING MUTUAL AID TO ADOLESCENTS

It is during the beginning stage that the adolescents in your bereavement group are introduced to mutual aid as a healing component. As they continue their grief journey, group members soon discover the meaning and importance of mutual aid, which has its foundations in social group work theory and whose activities and discussion topics are developed in accordance with what stage the group is in at any given moment. Building on this crucial concept of mutual aid, which can be defined as the process by which group members learn to help and support each other as they grieve the loss of their loved ones (Steinberg, 1997; Malekoff, 1997), the CBP has prepared a curriculum that is structured to enable the development of mutual aid. The singularities of the beginning stage of the group and the patterns established therein essentially dictate the rate of development of mutual aid. What is incontrovertible is that grieving adolescents need help in feeling connected to their group, in feeling that they share a common bond with the group experience, and in recognizing the group experience as a collaboration and a community effort. (For a more detailed discussion of mutual aid in Part I, see chapter 2.)

Activities and Discussion Topics That Build on Mutual Aid

The activities that are conducted and the topics that are discussed during the beginning stage of the adolescent bereavement group are steeped in mutual aid theory. They are intended to help the group members get to know one another and to begin to feel comfortable sharing with each other—sharing their own thoughts and feelings while at the same time allowing others to share theirs. The beginning activities allow the adolescents the opportunity to trust not only their fellow group members, but you as well, and the group process in its entirety. As you progress through the beginning stage and move on to the middle and ending stages, you will be using curricular activities that lend themselves to those stages, respectively. In other words, throughout the entire group process, you will be using activities and discussing topics that have been developed in accordance with which stage the group is in—beginning, middle, or ending (Kurland, 1982; Northen, 1988).

BEGINNING STAGE: DYNAMICS OF GROUP DEVELOPMENT

The following description of group development during the beginning stage has been adapted from the work of Roselle Kurland (1982) and is presented here with her permission. In the beginning stage of the group, adolescents experience a variety of emotions, which may include the following:

Anxiety about the unknown and uncertainty about what to expect

Inability to commit fully to the group and the tendency to exhibit some distance from the other group members

Conflicts between wanting to trust the group process and feeling suspicious and distrustful

Lack of readiness to jump right in, try new things, and reveal themselves

Dependence on you, their facilitator, for cues on how to act and what to say

Ambivalence about desiring closeness and acceptance while fearing rejection, embarrassment, and hurt feelings

Worry about failing and feeling vulnerable

Relief at taking that important first step in getting support

Ensuring a Successful Beginning Stage

Listed here are a few important objectives that you and your group members should strive to meet during the beginning stage:

You should discuss the purpose of the group with the adolescents and agree on the group's goals.

You should be able to connect with the group members.

The group members should be able to connect with you.

The group members should be able to connect with each other.

You should help the adolescents understand the group's orientation, including its structure, content, and logistics.

A Closer Look at Your Role as Group Facilitator

As the facilitator of your adolescent bereavement group, your role will evolve as you move from the beginning stage to the middle stage to the ending stage. Although teaching and learning rarely follow a perfect, straight path, you will notice that as your role changes, so will the roles and attitudes of the adolescents in your group. The following points provide more specifics about your role and responsibilities as group facilitator during the beginning stage:

To help establish a safe environment by reinforcing positive group norms and supportive behavior and discouraging norms that do not facilitate mutual aid—acting quickly and assertively in the process

To ensure that group members discuss, agree upon, and accept the purpose of the group

To discuss and explore expectations and responsibilities of group members

To assure adolescents that their feelings are perfectly normal for people who are just getting started in a bereavement group

To build and model trust by providing the group with structure, direction, and positive reinforcement when appropriate or necessary

To help group members to communicate and explore, at the same time showing them that you respect their need for distance

To express confidence in adolescents' ability to work together and achieve their goals as a group

To build connections between members by pointing out what they have in common

To facilitate the development of constructive group norms—both verbal and nonverbal—by modeling appropriate behavior and understanding purposeful use of self

Anticipated Outcomes

It is hoped that your bereavement group achieves the outcomes listed here. With your help as facilitator, adolescents should learn the following:

How to feel comfortable as they get to know one another, and how to feel just as much at ease as they get to know you and understand the group process, including group rules and confidentiality requirements

How to identify and normalize commonalities and differences between group members with regard to their experiences and feelings

How to discuss thoughts regarding death, including those that are affected by religion, culture, and family patterns of grieving

How to share personal experiences of loss, and how to listen to others as they share their loss, too

Feelings Sheet

OBJECTIVE   For group members to introduce themselves and establish commonalities and differences with regard to their feelings about the deaths of their loved ones

RATIONALE   During this opening session, some group members may feel reluctant to share their thoughts and feelings about their loss. That makes it all the more important for you to set the stage for the nurturing and celebration of respect, trust, and safety—components that are absolutely essential if your bereavement support group is to build a culture of mutual aid. Early in this session, after you explain your role as facilitator, you will introduce the concept of confidentiality and explain that it is a means to ensuring trust. You will also discuss the purpose of the group, its rules, and the type of behavior expected of the adolescents in the group.

This first activity in the 12-week curriculum begins the process of "normalizing" grief by identifying commonalities and differences between members. Group members should immediately be able to recognize that their feelings of grief and their reactions to it are not uncommon or unusual, nor are the feelings they have about taking part in the group's first meeting. They should be able to see that, along with the other adolescents in the group, they are not alone in their experiencing the normal and expected gamut of emotions in this brand-new environment.

Keep in mind the importance of emphasizing the need to create a respectful, supportive, confidential, and safe environment in which group members can feel comfortable sharing their grief with others, secure in the knowledge that they fit in with their peers and that their grief is normalized. During the first group, facilitators must check with each member to ensure that all information discussed in the group will remain in the group. By committing to doing this, members are starting out on the right foot as far as the process of trust is concerned. We have found that group members are respectful of one another and the loss of their loved ones. As a matter of fact, in all of our experience conducting bereavement groups, not once have we run into a problem concerning confidentiality.

MATERIALS

▷ 1 unmarked Feelings Sheet for each member and the facilitator (**p. 105**), plus an extra unmarked photocopy

▷ 1 blue fluorescent marker and 1 yellow fluorescent marker for each member and the facilitator

PROCEDURE

1. Personally welcome each adolescent to the group. Introduce yourself as the facilitator and explain the group purpose:

   "The purpose of this group is to help group members to give and receive support for the loss of a loved one."

2. Commend the members for joining the group. Explain that they have taken an important first step in dealing with their feelings of grief and say something such as the following:

   "By being here, you have made a commitment to yourself and to each other to participate actively in the process of grieving. Although you might feel worse before you feel better, I want you to know that we are all in this together and will help each other through this group process."

3. Tell the adolescents that in this group, certain rules must be followed. Solicit their suggestions for rules that will enable the group to work together. Make sure the following rules are included:

   We will respect each other.

   Only one person will speak at a time.

   All members have a right to be heard, and all members are expected to share their feelings about their loss.

   No one will be permitted to volunteer anyone else to share.

   Before having you take part in an activity, I will first model that activity so that the entire group has a sense of what is expected of them once we get started.

   Each time we meet, the group will begin on time and end on time.

4. Explain your agency's confidentiality clause to the group. We use the following:

"Everyone has heard about our 99 and 3⁄4 percent confidentiality clause. This is a reminder, in case you forgot: In our groups, members have what is called '100 percent confidentiality,' which means that everything said in the group remains in the group. However, as your facilitator, I have something else. It is called '99 and 3⁄4 percent confidentiality,' which means that if I hear something in the group that is alarming, such as certain members saying that they feel like harming themselves or someone else, or if certain members are being harmed by others, then I must contact someone at your school or at your home. But I will never do so without first informing you about it."

> By stating the confidentiality clause during the first group session, you are reminding group members that they are in control of whatever information they choose to share with you. You are also letting them know that if they tell you something that you feel is potentially dangerous to them or to others, then you will have to take action of some sort. When it comes to issues of confidentiality, there can be no ambiguity on your part as the group's facilitator.

Ask group members to acknowledge by nodding their heads that they agree to adhere to the confidentiality clause.

5. Begin discussing the difficulties inherent in the opening stage of any group and the general anxiety that accompanies them. Get the group to focus on the fact that they decided to sign up because they felt they needed help coping with the death of a loved one. This strategy will help to open the door for you, enabling you to explain your reason for wanting to act as group facilitator. It is here that you role-model by indicating that you, too, have had a personal experience of loss and related feelings.

    We advise you to wait until Week 2 to address any details about your loss.

6. Introduce and emphasize the importance of acknowledging and sharing feelings within the group as an essential means of giving and getting support. Ask all the members to share their reasons for joining the group.

7. Most members will say that their main reason for joining the group is to discuss their feelings. They will offer other reasons, too, and as they do, begin to synthesize these reasons into a smooth transition to the Feelings Sheet activity.

8. Holding up the unmarked copy of the Feelings Sheet so everyone can see it clearly, explain that the purpose of this activity is to

establish two things: (a) how the members feel about joining the group and (b) how they feel about the death of their loved one.

9. Point to each face on the sheet and make sure the group members understand the meaning of each feeling reflected in all the faces (e.g., happy, anxious, bored).

   Some of the feelings may have to be defined specifically for the group, such as "committed" or "miserable."

   Reassure everyone that all the feelings shown on the faces are normal and that there is no such thing as a "wrong" feeling. For example, one can feel happy about thinking about a loved one, or if a relationship was troubled, one may feel relieved.

10. Hand out one yellow marker and one blue marker to each member and explain that these markers will be used to highlight the group's feelings: The yellow marker will be used to highlight everyone's feelings about joining the group; the blue marker will be used to highlight everyone's feelings associated with his or her loss.

    Make sure all the group members understand that they can highlight as many or as few feelings that they have in either category, and tell them they can also highlight the same "feelings face" or "faces" in both categories. Thus, for instance, if they feel both thoughtful and curious about joining the group, they should highlight both the "thoughtful" and the "curious" faces with the yellow marker; if they also feel both thoughtful and curious about the loss of their loved one, they should highlight both the "thoughtful" and the "curious" faces with the blue marker.

11. As the adolescents complete their Feelings Sheets (a task that should take about 10 minutes or so), complete yours as well. Then go ahead and model your feelings about facilitating the group and explain your reasons for choosing each feeling.

12. Have group members take turns sharing their feelings about joining the group and explaining their reasons for choosing those feelings. Make a point of paying close attention to adolescents' choices and reasoning.

13. Solicit the group's observations about the commonalities and differences between them that were discussed as they shared their feelings, and then encourage them to continue sharing and discussing. You can offer your observations as well.

    Typically, adolescents will say they feel *excited, proud, anxious, curious, hopeful,* or *shy,* or any combination of these emotions. Although you will hear them mention an assortment of feelings, these are the ones we most commonly hear during this activity.

Be sure to reinforce the concept that all of the feelings they have are natural and expected—that there is no such thing as a "wrong" feeling.

Tell the group that they will revisit this activity in Week 11 of the ending stage and will no doubt find it interesting to compare their feelings near the end of the 12-week group to their feelings now, during the beginning of the group.

14. Once the adolescents have finished sharing and discussing their feelings associated with joining the group, go ahead and model your own feelings about the death of your loved one, and explain your reasons for choosing these feelings.

15. Have adolescents take turns describing their feelings about the losses they have experienced and explaining their reasons for choosing their feelings.

16. Discuss the wide range of feelings that the group is sharing:

Again, reassure members that all of their feelings are "OK."

Each member will have myriad feelings about his or her loss, and it is important that you acknowledge everyone's feelings, pointing out those that are similar and those that are different. Solicit the group's observations about the commonalities and differences among their feelings regarding the death of their loved ones.

The reason we divide the Feelings Sheet activity into two separate segments is to allow the group members to see that they have a lot in common when it comes to their thoughts and feelings about joining the group and with regard to the loss of their loved ones. Discussing the commonalities helps members to feel more connected to each other and hence more willing and able to share their most intimate and personal feelings about the loss of a loved one.

During both segments of the Feelings Sheet activity, you must listen very closely as the members give their responses. That way, you can accurately gauge the commonalities and differences among your bereavement group members.

17. Inform adolescents that in next week's session, they will be asked to introduce their loved one to their fellow group members. At this time, it is a good idea to address any concerns members may have about that. Some members may still be shy and therefore reluctant to speak up in the group meeting. It is your job to acknowledge that it is indeed difficult to share feelings in the beginning stage of any group. By reassuring members that their thoughts and feelings are both valued by the others in the group and valuable to the group's

mission, they will soon begin to feel taken care of, safe, and understood.

18. End the group session with a closing ritual that will be followed at the end of every session. At the CBP, we call it the "closing squeeze," although you or your group members may opt to choose a different ritual or a different name. In our closing squeeze, we hold hands, and one member begins by squeezing the hand of the member next to him or her. The squeeze is passed around the group until the final member receives the squeeze and says to the group: "Peace and be safe." Each week, a different group member begins the squeeze, and a different member utters the refrain. This way, everyone gets to play both roles.

Feelings Sheet

Name: _____ Date: _____

Happy	Anxious	Bored	Cautious	Confident	Angry
Committed	Confused	Curious	Don't Care	Frightened	Guilty
Hopeful	Hurt	Interested	Jealous	Lonely	
Miserable	Peaceful	Proud	Puzzled	Relieved	
Sad	Shocked	Shy	Sorry	Thoughtful	

Death Brainstorm Web

OBJECTIVE

Twofold: (a) For group members to use free association as they brainstorm thoughts, feelings, and images connected to the word *death* and (b) to begin the process of introducing their deceased loved ones to the rest of the bereavement group

RATIONALE

By taking part in the Death Brainstorm Web segment of the activity, group members benefit from brainstorming all words that come to mind upon hearing the word death, and also seeing it printed on a sheet of drawing paper in bold capital letters. As group members brainstorm words, they watch you write them down, and they see these words literally emanate, or radiate, from **DEATH,** which is centered on the page. Along with helping adolescents verbalize their feelings, this activity helps them to generate and recognize the wide range of thoughts, feelings, fears, and hopes associated with death that they share with their fellow group members.

The Death Brainstorm Web activity is a wonderful way to help adolescents gain confidence in speaking up and sharing their thoughts, and it also allows for a smooth transition to the second objective for Week 2: introducing to the group the loved ones they have lost through death. In this segment of the activity, group members verbalize the experiences of their loss, including the experience of losing the "relationship" they had with the loved one, and begin the mutual aid process of giving and receiving support from each other.

The Death Brainstorm Web activity enables the grief process for individuals and the group as a whole. As individuals, group members are asked to voice their personal associations with death. Thus, without feeling threatened, group members verbalize any and all thoughts and feelings they have regarding death. As a group, everyone acts as one in considering the feelings that have been shared individually. Because there are no wrong answers, the range of thoughts and images created by individuals in the group are automatically validated as normal. This activity facilitates the grief process by helping to allay group members' anxieties about what topics lie ahead in the ensuing 10 group sessions. An important bonus is that, once completed, the Death Brainstorm Web becomes a hands-on visual tool that recognizes and displays the wide array of ideas, topics, thoughts, and images that group members feel and visualize about death.

In its own way, the second objective for Week 2 also enables the grief process. In effect, it gives permission to group members to tell their stories about the relationships in their lives that no longer exist, at least on an earthly basis. In taking risks by sharing with others, group members open up their hearts and souls to each other. During this activity, group members can plainly see that they are not isolated in their experience of loss, and the pain and sadness that often accompanies it. This fact alone bonds the group and helps the mutual aid process to continue.

MATERIALS

▷ 1 large sheet of drawing paper and 1 thick marker for the facilitator

▷ Example of a completed Death Brainstorm Web **(p. 110)**

PROCEDURE

1. Ask the group whether they know what it means to brainstorm. If some or all of the members do not know what it means, explain it to them as follows:

   "To brainstorm means to say whatever comes to mind when, for example, you're asked a question or asked to comment on something you see. Brainstorming means that you do not edit, censor, or change in any way what you just said. In other words, it means that everything you say is correct because there are no wrong answers."

2. Introduce the first segment of the activity for this session and explain its purpose by telling adolescents the following:

   "Today we are going to do a brainstorm activity which will, in essence, be a guide to our discussions over the course of the next 10 weeks. I will write a word on this sheet of paper, and when you see it, I'd like you to say what first comes to mind."

3. On your large piece of drawing paper, use your thick marker and print **DEATH** in bold capital letters. Make sure everyone in the circle can see the boldfaced word, and then ask the group members to begin brainstorming.

   Be sure to tell the group not to raise their hands before they call out a word, as this slows down the process of brainstorming.

To help make it easy for you to conduct this activity, try to sit on the floor in the middle of the circle and write down the words as fast as you can.

4. As each adolescent calls out a word, be sure to draw a line that extends from **DEATH** and then—at the end of the line—print the word you hear so that, visually, the word appears as an extension of **DEATH.** (This process usually takes around 10 minutes.)

5. When there is a lull in the brainstorming, feel free to end the activity. But tell the group that your marker will rest on the paper for the duration of the session in case anyone would like to add any other words that come to mind when they see or think about the word *death.*

    Make sure that every member of the group calls out at least one word.

    As a facilitator, you understand that there are certain feelings and thoughts that are associated with death yet are not called out by group members; make sure you add them either during or after the brainstorming session. Among these words are the following: *dreams, nightmares, the afterlife, funerals, guilt, violence, hospitals, cancer, AIDS, fear, relief, anger, pain,* and *suffering.* It is up to you to know which additional feelings and thoughts that weren't mentioned are important enough to record on the Death Brainstorm Web.

6. Ask for a volunteer or two to read aloud the words that have been written on the Death Brainstorm Web.

    If no one volunteers, then read the words yourself.

7. End this segment of the activity by congratulating the group for working together to create the web. Point out the wide range of responses to the word *death,* and remind members once again that the Death Brainstorm Web will serve as a visual tool that guides them through the next 10 weeks.

8. Begin the second segment of the activity for Week 2—the introduction of loved ones—by telling the group the following:

    "Now we are going to take this opportunity to introduce our loved ones to each other. In order to support and better understand one another throughout the next 10 weeks, we need to know a number of things about everyone's loss experience: (a) who died, (b) how this person died, (c) when this person died, (d) what your relationship with this person was like, and (e) something you will always remember about this person."

Be sure to watch your wording when you ask members to introduce their loved one. Ask members to say something they will "always remember" about their loved one. Never qualify your request by asking for them to relate something good or something bad or even something special—just something they will always remember. It is up to the members to decide what they would like to share with the group.

Remind group members to be polite when others are talking and for everyone to look at one another when they are speaking.

Also remind members that it is OK to cry and to use the facial tissues when necessary. Be supportive and encouraging. If you feel it is necessary, walk over to a member and put your hand on the adolescent's knee or shoulder, but do not stop the adolescent from sharing. It is of the utmost importance that members know that it is fine to show emotion and that they will not be laughed at by anyone; on the contrary, they will be supported and understood. This activity often sets the mood for the group's future sessions because it helps to bond the members closely.

9. Model your own feelings about the loss of a loved one by answering questions (a) through (e). Remember that your modeling must be purposeful.

10. Ask who in the group would like to go first and share his or her story with the rest of the group, also answering questions (a) through (e). Group members will then take turns introducing their loved ones.

   Acknowledge that those who are listening to the story might have questions they would like to ask of the member who is speaking, but ask that they hold off and ask their questions after every group member has completed (a) through (e). This way, you will be ensuring that there will be time for each member to take a turn introducing his or her loved one to the group.

   Also acknowledge that, although members may have lost more than one significant person, because of time limitations, only one loved one may be introduced at this juncture. If time remains at the end of the group, you can ask members to introduce additional loved ones.

11. Once all the stories have been shared, ask the group if anyone has any questions to ask of each other's stories.

12. Point out similarities and differences among the stories that were told and thank the group members for being so courageous for sharing with the group.

13. End the group session with the closing squeeze.

Sample Completed Death Brainstorm Web

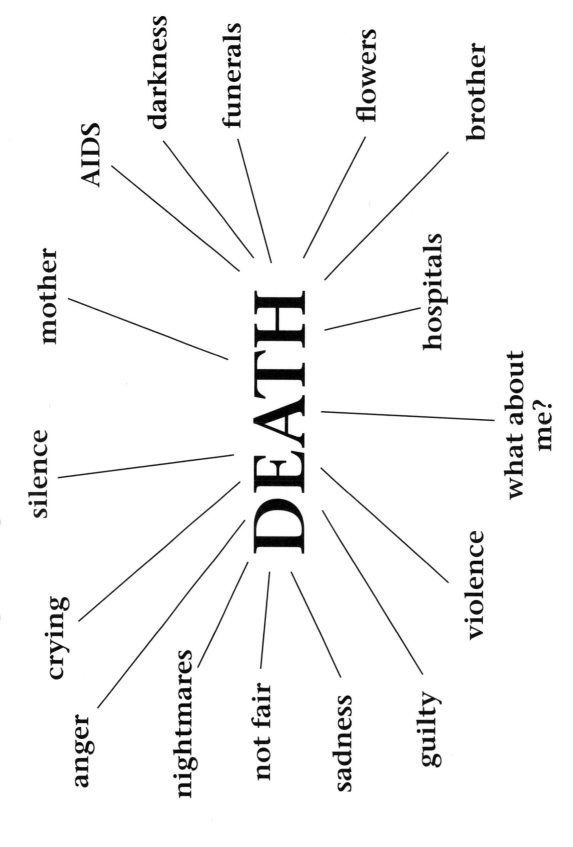

Guided Reflection through Visualization

OBJECTIVE   To use a creative visualization exercise to help group members think back on the death of a loved one, including the following aspects of their experience: how they were told about the death, whether the person or persons who told them about the death were supportive or unsupportive, their role and feelings at the funeral, and any regrets they may have about the loss

RATIONALE   This activity enables the grief process by allowing group members the opportunity to look back in time and recall vividly what happened during their loss experience. By providing a relaxed environment and then asking adolescents a series of questions that gently jog their memories, facilitators are able to help group members to "see" the events as they occurred at the time of the loss.

For some of the adolescents, this is the first opportunity they have had to express aloud the myriad feelings they have held inside for so long. Because they are being permitted to externalize previously internalized feelings, they are learning to create a sense of freedom for themselves—until now, an achievement many of them thought was unattainable. Although this newfound freedom opens the door to painful reminders and regrets, at the same time it allows members the ability to garner support from each other and to see quite clearly that they are not alone with their feelings of loss.

MATERIALS   ▷ The Guided Visualization Sheet for the facilitator (**p. 114**)

PROCEDURE   1. Introduce the activity and its purpose by telling the group the following:

111

"The purpose of the Guided Reflection through Visualization activity is to help you reflect on your experience of losing a loved one. In a little while, you will be able to close your eyes, relax, and listen to and answer a number of questions that I will ask you."

2. Tell the group that, even if they think they can't remember all of them, many different events took place before and after the loss of their loved one. You should then tell them the following:

"These events may include special things you did with your loved ones prior to their death or things you wished had not happened. You may also have memories of events that happened at the time of their death or afterward—at the funeral, for instance. There may even be things you wish you could have done differently either before or after your loved one's death."

Explain that by leading a guided visualization activity, you will help the group members reflect upon the memories of their loved one and the events surrounding their death.

3. Ask group members if they know the meaning of the word *reflect,* and even if they're not sure, to take a guess.

4. After exploring and discussing the various definitions that are offered by group members, explain that the meaning is to look back at the past and remember things that happened.

5. Begin the guided visualization activity by asking that group members shut their eyes and relax.

6. Ask members to close their eyes, stop talking, and relax their bodies as best they can. Then, speaking slowly and softly, read the questions from the Guided Visualization Sheet that appears on the last page of this activity.

When you ask the adolescents to close their eyes, stop talking, and relax, expect a few giggles at first. Be sure to explain that the reason you're asking them to do these things is to help them concentrate solely on their memories. Tell them that by closing their eyes and keeping quiet, they will not be faced with the problem of being distracted by other members' faces and voices.

7. Read the Guided Visualization Sheet to the group.

8. Invite the group to begin sharing their memories and ask who would like to be first to do so. Make sure you elicit memories from every group member. Tell the group they need not answer these questions in any particular order.

Because group members may be shy about beginning this discussion of memories, you may need to model some of your own memories to help jump-start the discussion. If that is the case, start by talking about your relationship with your loved one and continue from there.

Although you should always be prepared to model the activity that's being conducted, you will find that the adolescents in your group often have little or no trouble following your lead or acting on your prompt. Even at this early stage, many in your group will be starting to come out of their shells.

Many group members may believe that they could have done something to prevent the death from happening. When members start talking about regrets, make sure to normalize their feelings by reminding them that many people have regrets and that regrets are OK. Trying to persuade members that it is not their fault does not help them to feel better. Rather, talking about their regrets helps them to assuage their self-blame and guilt.

Keep in mind that your role as facilitator is to be empathic and to listen to group members so that they feel understood—not to tell them how to feel. You do need to be realistic, however, and help members to see the roles they did or did not play at the time of their loved one's death. Feeling sad because they did not go to the hospital the day their loved one died is normal, but it is not the reason the loved one died. Be sure to do a reality check with members so that they can put their regrets in the proper perspective. Members will then begin to follow your lead and confront such issues themselves.

9. After the discussion, commend your group members for taking risks and sharing such important memories with the rest of the group.

10. End the group session with the closing squeeze.

Guided Visualization Sheet

Think about your relationship with your loved one. What did that person mean to you? Were you happy with the relationship? If you could, would you do anything differently to change the relationship?

Now think back to how you were told about the death. Focus on where you were. Who told you? How did you respond? Were you able to show how you really felt?

Were any people particularly helpful to you at the time of the death? What did they do to make you feel supported? Were any people particularly unhelpful to you? How did they act toward you to make you feel unsupported?

Was there a funeral or other ceremony for your loved one? If there was, what was it like? Who spoke at the funeral? Did they accurately describe your loved one? What was your role at the funeral? Did you feel OK with the way the funeral turned out? Would you have done anything differently?

Most people have regrets when someone they loved dies. Do you have any regrets? Is there anything you wish had been different about your relationship with that person, with how you were told about the death, with the support you received from others, with the funeral, or with anything else involving your loved one's death?

I'm going to give you another few minutes to reflect on the death of your loved one, and when I ask you to, I'd like you to please open your eyes so that we can begin our discussion.

Without My Dad

OBJECTIVE   For group members to listen to the facilitator read a short story that was written by a peer—a story that highlights many of the issues involving the loss of a loved one—and then to discuss the themes that affect them personally

RATIONALE   This activity enables the grief process by giving members the opportunity to relate to the themes represented in the story. Listening to the story motivates group members to explore their own reaction to the loss of their loved one as well as the coping and adjustment processes that occur both at the time of the loved one's death and after. Because the facilitator is allowing for open-ended discussion, group members may choose to discuss some, many, or most of the issues highlighted in the story. This story may also serve as inspiration for group members to document their own story of loss and to memorialize it.

MATERIALS   ▷ "Without My Dad" **(pp. 119–121)**, a short story that the facilitator will read to the group

PROCEDURE   1. Explain to the group the following:

"The purpose of this week's activity is to highlight the many feelings, thoughts, and reactions a person may have when a loved one dies. The activity will entail my reading the following story to you as you sit back, relax, and listen intently:

"The story I will be reading to you is titled 'Without My Dad,' and was written by a 12-year-old named Lucy Yung, following the murder of her father. Lucy was born in Hong Kong and moved to the United States when she was 5 years old. She wrote this story while attending a bereavement group as a sixth grader."*

2. Tell the group to listen carefully for themes in the story that they can relate to. Remind them that, because everyone experiences different life stories, members are bound to relate to different themes. In other words, no two life stories are exactly alike. Inform them that, after you read the story, you will ask them to begin discussing the various themes that they could connect to the events in their own lives.

3. Read the story to the group.

4. Once you've finished reading the story, ask the adolescents to voice their thoughts about Lucy's experiences and to discuss anything else that her story brought to mind.

   After the reading, it may take a moment to get the group talking. Frame some questions in such a way that the adolescents will feel comfortable answering them and start thinking about themselves in relation to the book:

   > Ask if anyone in the group had any similar thoughts, feelings, or reactions to the news of their loved one's death.

   > If any group members lost a loved one to a violent act, ask if they had feelings similar to those of Lucy.

   Discuss the sudden-versus-anticipatory nature of loss.

   Many group members cry when they hear the last two lines of the story: "It was supposed to be a normal day like any other, but it turned out to be a nightmare I'll never forget. And my whole entire life had changed forever . . . . WITHOUT MY DAD." If some of the members cry, address the situation immediately by asking the following questions:

   > "Is that how some of you feel about the loss of your loved one?"

   > "Has your whole life changed forever?"

   > "How has your whole life changed forever?"

5. Ask members to discuss some of the themes they recognized in the story. Facilitate the discussion according to the responses you receive.

---

*Lucy Yung attended P.S. 158 in Manhattan and has since moved to Toledo, OH. She gave us permission to use her story and was glad to share it with other adolescents in bereavement groups because she found it to be a positive way to express her feelings and discovered that it helped her to heal from the pain of the grief she was suffering.

6. Although group members may touch on a variety of themes, they may have difficulty clarifying them or putting them into words. In our experience with adolescent bereavement groups who listen to Lucy's story, three themes seem to be most commonplace:

   In most of our groups, the theme that is addressed the most often is actually twofold, centering on guilt and regret (e.g., "Why did I fight with him . . . ?").

   Just as you did in Week 3, allow the group members to talk about this theme by normalizing rather than squelching their feelings. What often happens is that group members support each other despite their feelings of guilt and regret, and as a result, the members come to see that the thoughts and feelings that they have secretly held and carried inside are normal. It is important to note that—primarily because members are taking more risks and talking more openly about their innermost feelings—the discussion of this theme aids the transition from the beginning stage to the middle stage.

   The second most common theme that emerges from this story is that of religion and God. Some group members comment on this part of the text: "God will help. I go to church all the time and God said He will always be there when we need Him." Other members speak angrily about God, uttering something like "How could God allow something like this to happen?" Still others feel that God has helped them through their painful period. As group facilitator, your role is to listen to all of the differing thoughts and acknowledge all of them as valid.

   The third theme that most often arises pertains to one's initial reaction to the news of the death of a loved one—whether it is sudden or anticipated. Group members disclose feelings of shock, denial, and thinking that they were dreaming when informed of the death.

   To help facilitate more discussion, you can also talk about other themes, such as wanting to be strong for surviving family members and friends (e.g., not wanting to scare the baby), imagining a future without the loved one (e.g., "My life has changed forever"), and other short- and long-term changes associated with the death.

7. Keep in mind that as the discussion continues, it is important that you encourage all members to share and to make sure that they are talking with and looking at each other as they describe their thoughts and feelings.

8. Thank the adolescents for taking part in the activity and for supporting each other.

9. End the group session with the closing squeeze.

Without My Dad

by Lucy Yung

I can remember God said that good men always live longer than anybody else, and I believed it was true. My dad is the best in the world; everybody loves him. His friends always told me how lucky I was to be his daughter but I never realized that until now. He always cared about me, he cared a lot, but what I did was always fight with him.

I remember the day of October 9, 1992, a Friday. Just one of the normal usual days like any others. Like always I stopped in the restaurant, which is right next to where I lived, to see my hardworking father, who had provided me with all I needed and more. He was a man with a dream. The dream was to make the restaurant work. He even worked when it was 110 degrees inside. He worked and worked. I looked at him and saw a young man that looked like me. Flat nose and pulled eyes showing our Asian background.

All was well, and I left not knowing that that was the last time I would see him.

I got home, turned the key, and opened the heavy door. The first thing I heard was my baby sister crying. She was just born two months earlier. Sometimes it was very annoying, but sometimes it sounded like a song that would never end. Then I heard my mom calling me to do this, to do that, running back and forth like practicing for the track team in my school.

Finally, my mom finished her endless housework. And the baby fell asleep in my mom's arms. I don't know why, but it always makes me feel comfortable and safe, very protected.

Later I returned to my room, where it was so quiet and peaceful. It was where I always wanted to be, because I would always do what I want in my room, like read a mystery book (my favorite kind of book). Or do my homework while listening to classical music.

However, the day wasn't over. My mom was just putting the baby down in the baby's own bed, next to Mom's bed. She tried to rest, but at the same time she wanted to go down to the restaurant my dad owned. He had bought it 2 months ago after the baby was born. My mom wanted to help Dad because Friday was the most busy day of the week.

While Mom was getting ready to go to the restaurant, the phone rang. Mom picked it up quickly. She had a phone of her own, which I always wanted, but I never got one.

"Hello," Mom said.

I was thinking it was my friend Sayuri, who was calling to see if I was doing anything. Maybe she'd invite me to her house. Then I ran over to the phone.

But it seemed that something was wrong. My mom stood there, holding the phone down at her knees, making no sound at all. All of a sudden it was silent. I was wondering what happened. Then tears started running down her face slowly.

"What happened? What happened?" I yelled. She said, "Your uncle called and said—he said your dad was shot." I stood there, like my mom, not knowing what to say. I was scared to ask why. Then all of a sudden my mom took her coat, went down the stairs as fast as she could, and almost fell.

This is crazy. What's happening here? I asked myself. Am I dreaming? Well then wake up. My dad couldn't be shot by a gun. He cannot die. He can't just leave everything. What am I saying? It can't happen to me, to my family. What would I do without my dad?

It was unthinkable. I was already a girl of 12 years of age, almost grown up, but I could not imagine life without him. I know I am just dreaming . . . just dreaming.

So I slapped myself once, twice, three times. Then I realized I'm not—I am not dreaming at all, and I told myself to face it. God will help. I go to church all the time and God said He will always be there when we need Him. Later my sister wakes up and starts to cry again. I hold her in my arms like my mom would do. I was waiting nervously for my mom to call.

All of a sudden the phone rang. I was afraid to pick it up. Afraid of something bad. But I told myself it could be good news. I told myself not to worry. It was my second uncle. He called from the hospital.

"Is Dad all right?" I asked eagerly.

"Honey, I am sorry. . . he died during the operation," he said slowly and sadly. I stood there like before. Then I started to scream. I screamed so loud because I hoped maybe my screaming would make me feel better. This time it didn't help. I stopped because I didn't want to scare the baby.

Then I started to cry. Cry without a sound, just tears coming down, and I felt guilty. Why did I fight with him all those times and always get into arguments with him? Now I can't give anything back to him for all of what he gave me. Not even say sorry or goodbye. He just left. And no one would understand how bad or guilty I felt. And no one would know how much I really loved him, because all they saw were fights between us.

It was supposed to be a normal day like any other, but it turned out to be a nightmare I'll never forget. And my whole entire life had changed forever . . . .

WITHOUT MY DAD.

CHAPTER

8 Activities for the Middle Stage

The middle stage of the group becomes more complex for adolescents than the beginning stage, as group members begin to open up more readily and show their true selves (Kurland, 1982). In the hopes of determining whether they can trust what they see happening before them, group members may at this point try to test you and one another in a number of ways. Testing is what enables them eventually to use the group to its full potential and to enrich the bonds between everyone in the group, including you.

YOUR EXPANDING ROLE AS FACILITATOR AND YOUR EFFECT ON THE GROUP

During this stage, you should begin to pull back and allow the adolescents in your group to take more control; at the same time, you should continue to aid the development of positive group norms. As facilitator, your role is to help the group to resolve conflict rather than merely acknowledge it. This will require you to confront them whenever their behavior begins to stray from the group norm. As noted in chapter 7, your immediate response to aberrant behavior proves to the group that you value their need to feel safe and protected.

Changing Direction to Help Your Group Members Share More

Activities and discussion during the middle stage of group development require more intimate personal sharing. For both you and the group, this progression marks a distinct change in direction, for no longer are you relying on mere general discussions of topics of interest.

At this point your efforts should attempt to elicit from group members something more tangible than what they offered in the beginning stage.

By this time, group members have begun to identify what they have in common and can see more clearly what it is that sometimes separates and other times connects their experiences and feelings, depending on the situation. At this juncture, adolescents begin to communicate more easily with each other and learn to rely less on you and more on themselves for determining group structure. In the process, they continue to focus on normalizing their feelings of grief. These middle weeks also empower group members to feel comfortable describing the effects of the loss of their loved ones in a more multidimensional and somewhat variegated way; they begin to feel more at ease as they share both positive and negative memories.

MIDDLE STAGE: DYNAMICS OF GROUP DEVELOPMENT

The following description of group development during the middle stage has been adapted from the work of Roselle Kurland (1982) and is presented here with her permission.

At the *start* of the middle stage of the adolescent bereavement group, members are still dealing with the following:

Learning to feel comfortable and trying to fit in

Testing you, the other members of the group, and the group process

Figuring out trust issues

Trying to compete for attention, leadership, and power

Figuring out what their roles are in the group

During the middle stage, adolescents begin to do the following:

Challenge you by testing to see whether you really care about them and are committed to the needs of the group

Learn to depend less on you and more on each other

Express themselves more through sharing their experiences, ideas, and feelings

Take more positive risks

By the *end* of the middle stage, the following feelings are more prevalent among the adolescents in your group than they were at the end of the beginning stage:

Feeling comfortable being in the group

Feeling accepted and understood by the other group members

Being able to accept and understand the other group members

Being aware of the different group members' roles, including their own

Feeling that they understand the commonalities and differences between themselves and the other members of the group

Being aware of what they are contributing to the group

Being ready to share their personal experiences more openly and freely

Being able to care about the needs of other group members

Becoming aware of what the group is beginning to mean to them

Being able to develop realistic goals that can be achieved during group sessions

Being able to commend each other for taking risks and sharing

Ensuring a Successful Middle Stage

Listed here are a few important objectives that you and your group members will strive to meet during the middle stage:

Group members should begin to recognize and accept the group norms developed in the group (e.g., norms regarding communication, conflict, risk taking, social interaction, and support).

Group members should learn to develop interpersonal relationships within the group and understand how that affects the individual roles of members.

Group members should understand that the group's objectives need to be clarified and restructured so as to incorporate new goals that have been discussed by the group.

Group members should learn how to test you and their fellow members to determine that they can indeed take risks and be supported.

Group members should learn to respect the commonalities and differences between them that have arisen during the group up to this point.

A Closer Look at Your Role as Group Facilitator

As noted in chapter 7, your role as group facilitator evolves as your adolescent bereavement group moves from stage to stage. The following points provide more specifics about your role and responsibilities as group facilitator during the middle stage:

To aid the group as they tell their stories

To pull back and allow the group to take more control

To model and reinforce mutual aid and member-to-member communication

To use individual members' strengths and leadership abilities for the benefit of the group

To encourage the group to view conflict as an opportunity that enables them to improve and make progress

To monitor and evaluate the group's progress, especially with regard to communication, risk taking, and sharing

To discourage the development of subgroups, or cliques, within the larger group that may adversely affect the safety and mutual aid of the group

To address individual strengths, struggles, and progress within the group

To encourage the group to take ownership of the group process

To continue aiding the development and enactment of positive group norms

To observe commonalities and differences among members, and to connect them to the larger group's purpose and mission

To encourage members to be supportive and helpful and to listen to and hear each other

To allow the group to test you and each other without hurting members' feelings and jeopardizing the group's sense of safety

To allow adolescents to contribute to the group in their own unique ways

To confront the group as a whole or to confront individual members if their behavior strays from that needed to maintain the group norm and a safe haven

To validate members' feelings during group sessions, to regulate conflict, and to monitor communication patterns

To discuss concerns with individual group members outside of the group environment, as needed (e.g., to encourage expressiveness or to address a conflict)

Anticipated Outcomes

It is hoped that your bereavement group achieves the outcomes listed here. With your help as facilitator, adolescents should learn the following:

How to tell their stories and to explore the pain they feel

How to support group members as they remember their loved ones

How to discuss different forms of grieving a loved one, including rituals and memorializing

How to help the group to identify the changes in their lives and the reality of their existence since their loved one died

How to help group members reflect on their feelings of loss, including sadness, depression, and guilt

How to help group members to develop a connection with their loved one, focusing on memories, feelings, and experiences

Window to My Soul

OBJECTIVE

For group members to understand the following truism and to provide their own examples of it: (a) that bereaved individuals often present themselves in a certain way to the outside world, even though they may feel differently inside, and that (b) by using the medium of drawing, group members can show the differences between how they feel about their loss and how they portray themselves to others (e.g., to family, friends, and peers)

RATIONALE

The Window to My Soul activity that you will conduct during this session facilitates the grief process by giving group members the opportunity to explore the many different layers of self that they bring to the grieving process. Having members think about how they present themselves to the outside world and how they truly feel inside serves as a unique exercise that helps them to comprehend the universality of the grieving process. Through discussion, members begin to understand the reasons they present themselves one way to their peers and family members despite feeling a different way inside. By inviting adolescents to reveal their innermost feelings, you are enabling them to feel less isolated and better understood.

MATERIALS

▷ 1 Window to My Soul worksheet for everyone (p. 132)

▷ 1 orange

▷ Enough markers, colored pencils, crayons, or pastels for everyone

PROCEDURE

1. Introduce the activity to the group and explain its purpose, perhaps saying the following:

   "Today we are going to do the Window to My Soul activity, whose purpose is to help you to identify and explore the differences between how you present yourselves to the outside world in the aftermath of your loss and the way you really feel about it inside."

2. Introduce the idea known as "outside/inside." Give the group the orange, have them pass it around so every member has a chance to hold and examine it, and then ask them the following questions:

What is an orange like on the outside? How do you know?

What is an orange like on the inside? How do you know?

What purpose does the outside of the orange serve?

3. After getting feedback on the questions, make sure—once all is said and done—that the group understands that the purpose served by the outside, or the peel, is *protection*.

Note that you cannot see the inside of an orange because of the protective peel that covers it.

Explain to the group that there is a parallel between an orange and a human being: The outside part of a human being protects and conceals what is on the inside—for example, the private feelings one has upon losing a loved one.

4. Show group members the Window to My Soul worksheet. Explain that members will soon take part in the activity and (a) draw or write on the window shade how they feel they present themselves to the outside world concerning their loss and then (b) draw or write on the unshaded window how they actually feel inside concerning their loss.

This is probably a good time to reassure group members who may feel awkward or intimidated by the thought of having to draw. You can help them by reminding them that this is not an art activity.

5. Discuss and show samples of symbols and metaphors that other people have used in this exercise and explain what they mean.

In one example, a girl drew a beautiful blooming flower on the window shade; on the window she drew that same flower with all its petals scattered on the ground.

What do you think she was saying about herself?

In another example, a boy drew a calm ocean on the window shade and a tidal wave on the window.

What do you think he was trying to explain?

6. Reiterate to the group members that what we show on the window shade is *how we feel we present ourselves to the world* (i.e., the part

others see; what we want them to see as our visible self). What we show on the actual window, when the shade is up, is *how we are actually feeling inside* (i.e., the part that others rarely or never see, or the part of our inner self that we don't want them to see).

Make a point of clarifying that our inner selves may merely be different from our outer selves—not necessarily opposite, but nonetheless different.

Be sure to note that some members may feel that there is no difference whatsoever between their inner and outer selves. In other words, in their view, it doesn't really matter whether the window shade is up or down.

7. It is not uncommon for some members to be familiar with each other before their group's first meeting. How one friend perceives another friend is irrelevant. In other words, only the adolescents doing the activity can properly evaluate themselves.

8. Model the activity by showing the group how you have presented your window shade and window. As always, don't share too much. Keep in mind that you are simply modeling the activity.

9. Hand out the Window to My Soul worksheets and tell the group they have about 25 minutes to complete them. Assure everyone that you are available in the event that anyone needs help.

It's always a good idea for you to walk around the group and help those who are having trouble thinking of symbols and metaphors. If members are having difficulty, you might help them think of images that are relevant to their lives.

> For example, if a group member likes basketball, then you might help him or her to create a symbol using a basketball, a player, the court, or something similar.

Despite your reassurances in Step 4, you will still find yourself in the midst of some members who either don't want to draw or are too embarrassed to try. In those cases, have them write their ideas down in the places provided on the worksheet.

If members are not finished within the given time limit, make sure they know that what is most important here is the thought behind the activity.

Be firm, but polite, as you collect the pencils, markers, crayons, or pastels that the adolescents are using; otherwise, they might become so involved in the activity that they forget about the time limit and continue to draw after time is up. In some cases, adolescents may feel that they have to rush to get the job done.

Make sure you collect all the supplies; if you don't, some members in the group may be distracted by fiddling.

10. When group members have finished, ask for feedback on what it was like to do the activity:

   Was it hard to think about the way we see ourselves and the way we present ourselves to others?

   Were they able to find a symbol or metaphor to use for both their window shade and their window? How did they figure out what to use?

11. Instruct group members to share with each other while you facilitate the discussion.

   During this session, many group members often admit to feeling scared, vulnerable, hurt, sad, and sometimes even suicidal. Therefore, it is imperative that you not only be aware that an activity like this has the potential for bringing up repressed feelings, but that you keep your eyes open for any problems and be prepared to take action, if necessary.

   If group members talk of wanting to hurt themselves, ask them if they are thinking about it now, or whether they thought about it in the past. Ask other group members if they have felt the same way in the past? If they did, ask them how or whether those feelings passed. If a group member reveals to you feelings of suicide, ask him or her to stay after the group so that you can talk about it further. Have a suicide plan in mind so you can refer the member as you have been trained to do. Make sure you call the member's family (with the member's knowledge) to alert them to their child's feelings. Please note that in schools, you must tell the appropriate school official before anyone calls the child's parent or guardian.

12. Congratulate group members for the enormous risks they took by sharing such intimate and private parts of themselves with each other.

13. End the group session with the closing squeeze.

Window to My Soul

Name: _____ Date _____

How I present myself to others . . .   How I feel inside . . .

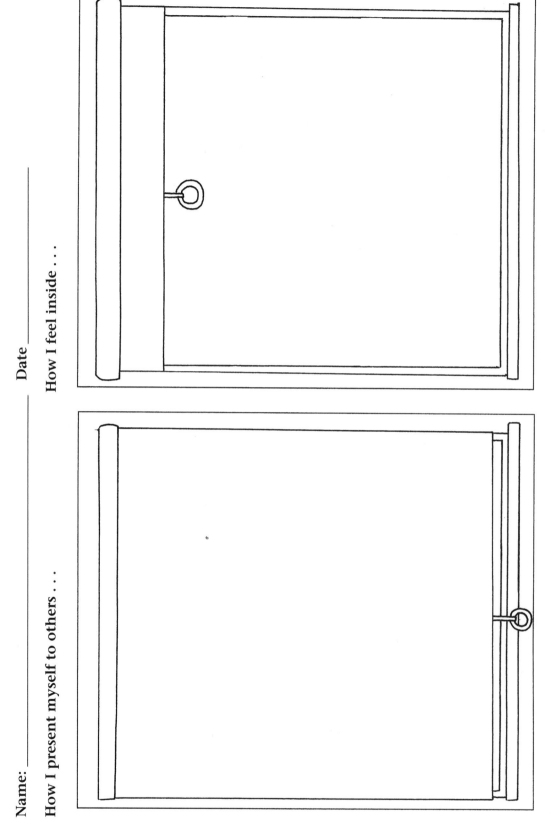

Grieving, Sharing, and Healing: A Guide for Facilitating Early Adolescent Bereavement Groups
© 2005 by Rekha Murthy and Lisa-Loraine Smith. Champaign, IL: Research Press (800) 519-2707

132

Memorial Poem

OBJECTIVE To help group members recall and share memories of their loved ones, both positive and negative, commemorating them forever with a Memorial Poem that uses a worksheet and a structured format

RATIONALE In a departure from earlier activities, which have focused primarily on the loss experience (i.e., feelings and events having to do with the death), the Memorial Poem gives group members an opportunity to recollect the lives and the qualities of their loved ones.

Reminiscing is an essential process of grief because our memories allow us to feel connected to our loved ones and to remember joyful as well as bleak moments. Young people often say they feel sad when they think about their loved ones. This activity empowers group members to take ownership of their memories and to share them within the safe environment of the bereavement group.

By recalling their loved one's qualities—specific likes, dislikes, and hopes—group members begin to see their loved one emerge as a whole person, separate from the adolescent. Because it is common for young people to glorify a loved one after death, this activity enables group members both to remember and to create a memorial of the loved one that captures the "real" person. Therefore, the creation of a Memorial Poem gives group members a permanent and tangible object to hold onto and also allows them to memorialize their recollections. As a result, group members learn how to integrate the loss into their lives by focusing realistically on their memories.

MATERIALS ▷ 1 Memorial Poem worksheet (**p. 138**) for everyone

▷ 1 pen or pencil for everyone

▷ Enough markers or crayons for every group member

PROCEDURE

1. Explain the purpose of the activity by telling the group the following:

   "We are going to do an activity today, the purpose of which is to write a Memorial Poem that recalls the memories you have about your loved one. The purpose is to think about the memories you have of the person, both positive and negative, and to create a poem that uses those memories in a way that memorializes the loved one."

2. Discuss the importance of memories we have—both positive and negative—when we lose a loved one: Explain that sometimes our memories can make us sad, but that recalling them allows us to make the loved one a part of our lives.

3. Discuss the purpose of creating a memorial.

   Ask the group the meaning of the word *memorial* and to think about any examples they may have seen, such as an AIDS quilt.

   Explain that, shortly, everyone will be writing a Memorial Poem.

4. Holding up the Memorial Poem worksheet, explain that group members will use the worksheet to create their poems, which they will share with the rest of the group at the end of the session.

   Some adolescents may feel anxious about writing a poem: They may dislike writing, or they may be under the impression that all poems should sound a certain way. You can help them by spending a few moments talking about poetry as a way of creating an image through words and by explaining that the Memorial Poem is no different because it will include group members' memories and therefore create an image of their loved one.

   Reassure group members that the simple structure of the poem will enable everyone to successfully complete this activity.

   Recognize those instances in which you may have to assist certain members who have limited literacy skills by working with them individually.

   Group members with limited memories of their loved ones may also require special support.

   > If group members had minimal contact with their loved one, for example, or if they were too young to remember them, then evoking memories may be difficult.

   You may wish to meet with members you identify as having the difficulties mentioned here during the previous week.

If these adolescents have relatives or friends who knew the loved one, perhaps they can help the members to do the activity beforehand.

In situations where members who are having difficulties do not know anyone who can help them, try having the member imagine what the loved one was like.

5. Tell the group members that their poems will consist of 11 lines that follow a pattern. At this point, you should hand out the worksheets to the adolescents and then go through each line of the poem, explaining and giving examples for each line, as follows:

Line 1: First name of the loved one

Group members write the first name of the loved one.

Line 2: Four characteristics that describe the loved one

Group members write four adjectives that describe the loved one (e.g., caring, tall, protective, patient).

Line 3: Role in the family of the loved one

Group members describe one or more roles the loved one played in life (e.g., mother, uncle, brother, the one who actually liked washing the dishes, my best friend).

Line 4: who loved

Group members write the hobbies and passions of the loved one. Here, "who loved" is not meant in the romantic sense, but rather in the following sense (e.g., "who loved dancing salsa, hanging out with friends, living dangerously, playing video games").

Line 5: who felt

Group members describe their perception of the loved one's feelings in life (e.g., "who felt happy when he was with me, proud to be my father, understanding whenever I was sick").

Line 6: who needed

Group members describe their perception of the loved one's needs in life (e.g., "who needed a bigger house, lots of hugs, love, better health, good luck, more money").

Line 7: who gave

Group members describe what the loved one gave to them or to others in life (e.g., "who gave presents, love, good advice, attention").

Line 8: who feared

> Group members describe their perception of the loved one's fears in life (e.g., "who feared not being there for his kids, the effects of drugs and violence, nothing, God").

Line 9: who envisioned

> Group members describe, after you define the word *envision,* their perception of what the loved one visualized or thought might happen in life (e.g., "who envisioned becoming a teacher, seeing her grandchildren graduate high school, traveling home to Puerto Rico").

Line 10: who is a resident of

> Group members describe their ideas of where the loved one is or where the memories of the loved one are ("a resident of my heart, of my dreams, of Heaven, of Earth").

Line 11: Last name of the loved one

> Group members write the last name of the loved one.

6. Go ahead and model your Memorial Poem. When you read your poem aloud, do not read the words that appear in parentheses on the worksheet (i.e., first name, four descriptive characteristics, role in the family, and last name).

Once the group members have asked any questions they may have, they can begin writing their own Memorial Poems. Before they begin, though, offer them a few suggestions and reminders that may help them:

> Encourage them to think of several examples for each line of the poem, if possible.

> Let them know that both concrete and abstract responses are acceptable and encouraged (e.g., concrete: who loved music; abstract: who loved living life fully).

> Tell them that they are not required to complete the Memorial Poem in the order that the lines are presented; tell them they can skip around until they have completed the activity.

> Reassure them that you will be happy to help them if they run into any problems.

7. After the group members have completed their poems, go ahead and process the activity. Ask the group to reflect on the activity by asking them the following:

What was it like for you to do this activity?

Was it difficult or easy to remember your memories?

Were certain lines easier or harder than others? If so, which ones?

What feelings did this activity bring up for you?

Was it a challenge to think about your loved one in this manner?

8. Have group members share their poems with the rest of the group.

    If certain members feel uncomfortable in any way, they can choose to read only a portion of their poem or ask you or another member to help them read it. However, encourage them to share their entire poem, if possible.

    > It is extremely important, however, that all members share so that the common bond of the group is strengthened and reinforced.

9. If time permits, encourage group members to use their markers or crayons to decorate their Memorial Poems. We usually type up the members' poems so that both the original Memorial Poem and the typed Memorial Poem can be placed in the folders containing their work, which will be returned to them during Week 11.

10. Inform the adolescents that in the activity the following week (Week 7), the group will be sharing photos and other treasures of their loved one.

    Explain that a treasure is any object that holds sentimental value for group members when they think about the person who died.

    > If a group member reports not having any photos or treasures, explain that he or she can make and share a drawing or a treasured memory with others in the group.

    Remind group members to bring their treasures the following week.

11. End the group session with the closing squeeze.

Memorial Poem

(First name of the loved one) _____

_____

(Four characteristics that describe the loved one) _____

_____

(Role in the family) _____

_____

who loved _____

_____

who felt _____

_____

who needed _____

_____

who gave _____

_____

who feared _____

_____

who envisioned _____

_____

who is a resident of _____

_____

(Last name of the loved one) _____

_____

Treasures from the Past

OBJECTIVE To help group members reminisce and discuss memories of their relationship with their loved one by encouraging them to share with the rest of the group the pictures, mementos, and other treasures connected with the loved one that they were asked to bring to the Week 7 session

RATIONALE Week 6 marked the beginning of the discussion of the importance of memories and focused on recollecting the life and qualities of each group member's loved one. Week 7 continues this process by allowing group members to use pictures and objects to fortify their memories of their relationship with the person who died. Photos and other treasures serve to make real the descriptions group members shared in Week 6 regarding the deceased. Cherished objects such as these help everyone to feel closer and better connected to the loved one we are focusing on and stand as concrete evidence of the relationship we had with that person as well as the one we continuously strive to maintain through our memories.

MATERIALS ▷ Group members' pictures, letters, mementos, and other treasures connected with their loved one

PROCEDURE 1. Explain to the group the purpose of the activity by telling them the following:

"We are going to do an activity today called Treasures from the Past. The purpose of the activity is to share with everyone in the group a collection of pictures, letters, mementos, and other treasures that strengthen our memories of our loved ones and help us remember how much we valued our relationships with them."

2. Model by sharing your treasure first; then have group members take turns sharing their treasures with the group, explaining to the others their significance and also sharing memories of their relationship with the loved one.

3. Depending on the flow of the discussion, you may choose to open up other topics for discussion or continue previous discussions. At this time, for instance, you may wish to reintroduce the Death Brainstorm Web activity from Week 2—or any activity, for that matter—as a means of reinforcing discussion and encouraging adolescents to reflect on their group experience.

Because the group will be passing the midpoint of the 12-week curriculum, they will have reached a juncture at which they feel much safer than they did during the beginning stage. The Treasures from the Past activity is particularly beneficial because it is fairly unstructured and takes the form of an open discussion, with adolescents sharing their cherished items.

Another plus is that, for those members who could not find tangible items to bring to the session, they will feel more comfortable than they did in earlier activities to talk about their loved one, to describe and share memories and stories of the person with their fellow group members. They can even draw a portrait of the person at home prior to the session—just as long as they know that a treasure is any object that carries significance or sentimental value for the young person (e.g., a gift, a birthday card, an article of clothing).

Keep in mind that not all group members will have only pleasant memories of the deceased. Therefore, you should make it clear that adolescents are free to discuss both positive and negative experiences as they share their mementos and photos.

4. End the group session with the closing squeeze.

Letters to Loved Ones

OBJECTIVE   To help group members compose a letter to their loved one, writing whatever they want to so that it enables them to feel more connected to the person, and then sharing the letter with the rest of the group

RATIONALE   This activity facilitates the grieving process by helping group members to feel connected with the lost loved one in a unique way. The purpose of the activity is not to have group members offer a permanent goodbye to their loved ones; rather, it is about helping group members to say anything and everything they may want to say to their loved one, or to say anything they wished they had said when the loved one was alive.

The Letters to Loved Ones activity helps group members to understand that their thoughts, feelings, and memories regarding their loved ones will never be completely lost to them. Writing this letter allows them to express, concretely, feelings such as guilt, regret and hope to the loved one, enabling them to incorporate the relationship they had with the loved one into their current life. It also sets the stage for the Balloon Release activity in Week 9.

MATERIALS   ▷ Enough light-colored stationery for everyone

▷ A ballpoint pen for everyone

▷ The facilitator's model letter

▷ The Balloon Release Permission Request (written by the facilitator on agency letterhead)

PROCEDURE   1. Introduce the activity and its purpose by telling the group the following:

"We are all going to write letters to our loved ones today and share them with the entire group. The purpose of this activity is for all of us to be able to say whatever we want to our loved one. Oftentimes, when we experience a death, we may be afraid to think about or remember the loved one. As a result, we may try to bury our memories of the deceased and avoid talking about him or her. Writing this letter enables us to take a step toward bringing our loved one and our memories back into our lives, toward creating a way to continue our relationship with the loved one."

2. Inform the group that the letters they write today will eventually be placed inside helium balloons that they will release as part of the following week's activity.

   Remind the adolescents that this activity is, in essence, a form of communication with their lost loved one, but keep in mind that the process of writing such a letter and then releasing it in a helium balloon might run counter to some members' religious beliefs.

   > In these cases, ask the members if it's OK for them to write *about* their loved one rather than *to* their loved one. Whatever their decision, assure them that they may opt not to release their balloons in Week 9—and that you and the group members will support their choice and respect their right to do what they need to do.

3. Engage the group in a brief discussion of the different things they might include in their letters.

   At the CBP, we have had success beginning with the question, "What would you want to say to your loved one if he or she were here now?"

   > Adolescents may choose a number of options: They may, for example, want to "update" their loved one on their current life events—what grade they are in, whether they like their school, who their friends are, how the rest of the family is doing, who got married, who had a child, who died.

   > Other important topics that adolescents may want to include in their letters are discussions of any regrets they may have; an exploration of their feelings about the death of the loved one; a story or particular memory of the loved one; or a recollection of how they believe the loved one felt about them, including what positive attributes of theirs they felt were appreciated and celebrated by the loved one.

4. Share your own letter to your loved one, which you wrote sometime prior to today's session, and read it to the group.

5. Hand out the stationery and writing utensils to all the members and have them write their letters, allowing them about 25 minutes to complete the activity.

   To alleviate any of the group's fears as they write their letters, reassure them that the length of their letters is unimportant. They can be as short or as long as members desire—from a single paragraph to several pages.

   As always, stay consistent by making yourself available to answer questions and to offer encouragement and support to adolescents during the writing process.

6. When the group is finished writing, explore with them what it felt like to write the letter:

   Was the letter difficult to begin?

   Were some parts easier or harder to write about than others?

7. Have group members share their letters. Although you should encourage them to read their entire letter, they should at least read a portion of it.

   As facilitator, you should recognize the risk that is involved here for certain members, yet at the same time you must understand the importance of everyone's sharing. If everyone shares except for a few members, then the atmosphere in your group will be unbalanced. To help prevent this, you should solicit a volunteer to initiate the sharing.

   As you can see, this activity is crucial to the promoting and strengthening of mutual aid. That's why it's important that group members are encouraged together to take the risk involved in this activity. Frequently, members use their letters to disclose previously unrevealed personal information. This makes it all the more important for each member to feel safe and to work together to support each other during this intimate process.

   After the group members have shared their letters, have them hand them to you so that—prior to Week 9—you can use a photocopier to reduce them roughly to the size of a computer disk so that they will fit inside a balloon. Fold the letters accordion-style, and then in half again, making sure that the words appear on the outside. Collect letters for safekeeping until Week 9, when they will be placed inside the helium balloons.

8. Make sure you help the group to explore and discuss what it was like to share and to hear others' letters.

9. Before the end of the session, be sure to ask each member what color balloon he or she prefers (Allow everyone in the group to make a

first and second choice of colors). If more than one member picks the same color, tell the individuals that a different-colored string can be used to differentiate their balloons. Keep track of which color each member chooses.

Establish a relationship with a stationery store or any store that sells and uses helium balloons by explaining the program and the purpose of the activity so that they will insert the letters in the balloons and then blow up the balloons with helium. Make sure they know to have the balloons ready for you to pick up on the day of the Balloon Release activity (Week 9).

Let the group members know that you have decided on an appropriate location for the group to release their helium balloons (preferably somewhere nearby and easily accessible). Ideal locations include neighborhood parks, nearby courtyards, and school yards.

> *Remember to get permission from the appropriate authorities—including, perhaps, school officials and parents or guardians—before taking the group to the location for the balloon release in Week 9.*

10. Hand out to all members the Balloon Release Permission Request and tell them to have their parent or guardian sign it, and bring it back to the group the following week.

     If any member was absent today, and thus unable to write a letter, you will need to telephone that member before Week 9 and inform him or her of the activity and its purpose. If possible, the adolescent should write the letter regardless, and read it to the group at the release site in Week 9. If a photocopier is accessible on the day of the balloon release, you can reduce it. You can then bring the member an empty balloon (if possible, of the color chosen by the adolescent) and simply tie the miniature letter to the balloon string to be released.

11. End the group session with the closing squeeze.

Balloon Release Permission Request

(Written on Agency Letterhead)

Date: _____

Dear [Parent or Guardian]:

The bereavement support group that your child is attending is progressing well. We are currently in our eighth week together and will continue to meet for the next four weeks. As part of this week's activity, the group members have written letters to their loved ones who have died. These letters will be placed in helium balloons and released into the sky next week (Week 9). As the group's facilitator, I would like to take the group members to [location], where we will release the balloons during our regular meeting period. Please sign below to give your child permission to leave the school building, under my supervision, for about 30 minutes next week. Thank you, and please do not hesitate to call me at the phone number below if you have any concerns or questions.

Sincerely,

_____

[Title]

[phone number]

I give _____ permission to attend the balloon release activity with

the bereavement group on _____.

Signature: _____

Relationship: _____

CHAPTER

9   Activities for the Ending Stage

The ending stage of the adolescent bereavement group triggers the range of feelings group members feel about loss. Because the curriculum is structured so that members are encouraged to reflect on their group experience, activities and discussion center on examining their lives up to this point, contemplating what they have experienced in the bereavement group, and looking toward the future and what it might hold.

ENDING STAGE: DYNAMICS OF GROUP DEVELOPMENT

The following description of group development during the ending stage has been adapted from the work of Roselle Kurland (1982) and is reprinted here with her permission. In the ending stage of the adolescent bereavement group, members often do the following:

Communicate more openly than before because they feel more comfortable by the time they reach this stage

Begin to develop relationships with group members outside the group environment

Discuss how the group changed over time and how individual members grew

Feel ambivalent, anxious, or disappointed about the group's impending termination

Regress by acting in a way that typifies behavior more commonplace in the beginning stage

Fail to show up for group meetings, perhaps in an unconscious attempt to leave the group before the group leaves them

Fear the loss of support once the group ends, knowing they will no longer be able to interact in the group with you and their fellow members

Ensuring a Successful Ending Stage

Listed here are a few objectives that you and your group will strive to meet during the ending stage:

You should address issues concerning the group's termination and discuss them with the adolescents.

You should help group members explore ways in which—after the group is terminated—they can remember and preserve the positive changes that the group created.

You should help the group members feel supported despite the group's termination.

A Closer Look at Your Role as Group Facilitator

As discussed in chapters 7 and 8, your role as group facilitator evolves as your adolescent bereavement group moves from stage to stage. The following points provide more specifics about your role and responsibilities as group facilitator during the ending stage:

To process the feelings members have about the group's termination

To encourage members to think about and discuss any regrets they might have about their participation in the group, and to have them talk about any goals they felt that they or the group did not achieve

To help adolescents evaluate the overall group experience

To make a point of noting both individual and group progress that you observed throughout the three stages of the bereavement group, and to express confidence in members' ability to continue to make progress after the group is terminated

To discuss the nature of follow-up, as it is applied by the host agency

Anticipated Outcomes

It is hoped that your bereavement group achieves the outcomes listed here. With your help as facilitator, adolescents should learn the following:

How to identify unresolved feelings and regrets

How to acknowledge connections made with their loved ones

How to release painful feelings after the group has completed its work

How to share feelings of termination and loss as the group ends and how to evaluate the group process

How to think about their lives beyond the death of their loved one and toward their future goals

How to continue discussion about death, especially the handling of future losses

How to explore their strengths and struggles so that they can recognize what is important to them in their lives

How to recognize any needs they have for ongoing support and follow-up services provided by the host agency or any other organization

Balloon Release

OBJECTIVE

To help group members symbolically release their thoughts and memories of their loved ones, and at the same time strengthen their connection to their loved ones and to the group as a whole, by releasing helium balloons containing the letters they wrote in Week 8

RATIONALE

Writing their letters in Week 8 offered group members an opportunity to express their thoughts and emotions to and about their loved ones and to maintain a connection with them. By releasing the letters symbolically in Week 9, they fortify this connection by "sending" their letters to their loved ones. In the process, they also begin to take more control over the grieving process.

MATERIALS

▷ Helium balloons containing letters written by everyone the previous week, including the facilitator

PROCEDURE

1. On the day of the Balloon Release activity, before arriving at the session site, pick up the group's helium balloons from the stationery store or other vendor.

   As discussed in Week 8, the miniature letters should already have been reduced on a photocopier and folded accordion-style—and then in half again—with the words of the letters facing outward.

   The letters (including yours) should already have been inserted in the balloons and the balloons inflated with helium by the vendor, per your instructions. Because the helium will begin to escape from the balloons in about a day, make sure the vendor has them ready for you the day you stop by to pick them up—and that the balloons were inflated as recently as possible.

Make sure you have kept track of which balloons belong to which adolescents. Use a system that's based on a color scheme—including the color of the strings, if necessary.

2. When you meet with your group here in Week 9, introduce the activity and its purpose by saying the following:

   "We are going outside today, where we will be releasing the helium balloons containing the letters you wrote last week. As mentioned last week, the purpose of this activity is to release symbolically to your loved ones your thoughts and feelings about them."

3. Engage the group in a discussion of faith, the afterlife, dreams, spirits, traditions, and rituals. Ask them questions such as these:

   Where do you think your loved one is now?

   Where do you think the balloons will go?

   What are your and your family's beliefs about religion, God, and customs?

   > (Following up on the previous question) Do you or your family have particular rituals or traditions that you observe to help you remember your loved one?

4. In the group setting, helping adolescents come up with creative rituals facilitates their memory of the person who died, particularly on meaningful days, such as the loved one's death anniversary or birthday or any other day that carries significance.

   It is important to remind the group that everyone has different beliefs regarding the issues being discussed, and that their feeling safe and respected are essential to the success of the group.

   Note that, symbolically, the balloons go wherever every member wants them to go. It is therefore important to reinforce that everyone's beliefs are correct and are supported by the entire group.

5. Before the group departs the premises to begin the activity, they must decide how they want to release their balloons once they reach the release site.

   For example, they may choose to stand in a circle and release their balloons one at a time, or they may choose to release them simultaneously.

   In a variation on that theme, they may prefer to stand in a circle and take turns reading their original letters one more time before releasing their balloons—either one at a time or simultaneously. Make sure to bring the original letters with you.

Another possibility is for them to utter a few spontaneous words beforehand (e.g., "Dad, I miss you, and I wish you were here" or "Mom, I hope you get this letter, wherever you may be") and then release the balloons all at once or one at a time.

Group members may even wish to recite a short poem or prayer before releasing their balloons.

Numerous options are available; what is important is that the group devise a solid plan before arriving at the release site, thus making the actual release the focal point of the activity once the members arrive at the site.

In the end, what it comes down to—what needs to be understood—is that this popular, revered activity offers the group a wonderful opportunity to work together and to act together as one.

> The activity allows the group to think collectively about the bonds of fellowship that hold them together and at the same time allows for individuality: They are all sending messages to their loved ones, and each of their messages is unique; thus every adolescent's religious and philosophical beliefs are integrated into the circle and respected by everyone.

6. Once a definite plan has been reached, go over your agency's rules for safe travel, and have the group join you in proceeding to the release site.

The group can choose to have you carry all the balloons, or members can carry their own balloons. However, urge them to be careful, as the balloons are fragile and may pop, if mishandled. If a balloon pops on the way to the release site, the group member can tie his or her letter to the string of another member's balloon, and the two of them can be released in tandem.

7. After arriving at the site, follow the agreed-upon procedure.

Once you are certain that the group is ready to begin, have everyone follow the plan and release the balloons.

If you wish to, feel free to recruit a volunteer to begin the ceremony while you participate according to the plan that everyone developed. If the group would rather you model first, that is fine, too.

It is important for group members to be aware of how everyone is feeling and to support one another: Feelings of sadness, hope, anxiety, uncertainty, relief, connectedness, and a host of others are all common.

If a group member is absent on the day of the balloon release, you can help by releasing the absent member's balloon yourself or tying it to someone else's.

Be aware that you may need a backup location in mind—such as the school yard or simply outside the host agency, if not at a school—should inclement weather pose a problem.

8. Once the balloons have been released, the group may decide to remain at the site until they can no longer glimpse any trace of the balloons. This is a perfect opportunity for you to check in with the group and process their thoughts and feelings about the activity.

    The Balloon Release activity is usually considered the high point for group members during the entire 12-week curriculum; they appreciate the symbolism of the activity and like to talk about it. The Balloon Release activity begins the process of enabling the group to make a smooth transition from the middle stage to the ending stage.

    The activity also prompts group members to think seriously about how they have progressed since the beginning stage. They begin to discuss with increasing frequency the shared strengths and struggles they have experienced, and they also come face-to-face with the realization that the group will soon come to an end.

9. Return to the school building and end the session with the closing squeeze.

Looking Backward . . . Looking Forward

OBJECTIVE   For group members to write a three-part poem that enables them to reflect on past events that have influenced them, to think about the present and where their life path has taken them thus far, and to look toward the future and what they hope to accomplish

RATIONALE   This session facilitates the grief process by helping group members to view their losses in the larger context of their life paths. Up to this point, group members have focused on their loved ones and their accompanying loss experience. This activity, while still incorporating the loss experience, enables the group to go beyond their losses to explore other facets of their lives.

By taking part in this activity, group members are given the opportunity to stop and think more clearly about their lives and to see how their losses, their childhood, and the group experience have shaped the people they have become. In the process, they learn to share their dreams and hopes for the future, which in turn enables them to see that their losses are merely a part of a longer, more winding life path—one which encompasses a past, present, and future. In the end, this activity helps group members realize that they can retain their memories of and their connection with their loved ones, while simultaneously moving forward in their own unique lives.

MATERIALS

    ▷ 1 Looking Backward . . . Looking Forward worksheet for each group member **(p. 158)**

    ▷ A pen or a pencil for each group member

    ▷ The facilitator's copy of the Looking Backward . . . Looking Forward worksheet (completed prior to the session)

PROCEDURE

1. Introduce the activity and its purpose by telling the group the following:

   "We are taking part in an activity today called Looking Backward . . . Looking Forward, which will allow us to think about our lives—in the present, in the past, and in the future. The purpose is to think about our life paths as well as some of the different people and events that have influenced who we are now and our hopes for the future. We will look backward and then forward, thinking about our childhood, our loved ones, our group experience, and our individual selves and personal goals."

2. Take a few minutes to discuss with the group the metaphor, or analogy, represented by a life path. Show them that we are all on our own unique life path, each one shaped by different people and events, different strengths, and different struggles. Ask them the following:

   What does our current life path look like (e.g., as it relates to school, friends, home, loss)?

   Thinking back, what does our past life path look like (e.g., recalling elementary school, childhood)?

   Can we envision our future life path (e.g., as it relates to experiences with high school, career, marriage, personal dreams, and goals)?

3. Holding up a blank Looking Backward . . . Looking Forward worksheet, explain that the three columns represent the three different elements of our life path—our past, present, and future—with the footprints used as a visual aid to symbolize our life path:

   The "I remember . . ." column refers to our past.

   The "I am . . ." column describes the person we are now.

   The "I hope to . . ." column refers to our future hopes and dreams.

4. When thinking about the three columns on the worksheet, adolescents should reflect on four different aspects of their life experience: the loss of their loved one, their group experience, their childhood, and their future goals. Some typical statements follow:

   The "I remember . . ." column can incorporate memories of their loved one ("I remember laughing with my grandma as we ate dinner"); memories of their childhood ("I remember the first time I went to Disney World"); and memories of the group experience ("I remember watching the whole group release the balloons"). Included in their memories can be people, events, things, places, special moments, and the like.

The "I am . . ." column describes the group members' qualities, beliefs, interests, feelings, identities, and more. Again, they can incorporate their loss experience, group experience, and their sense of self (e.g., "I am lonely at times without my father"; "I am proud that I joined this group"; "I am Dominican"; "I am an artist").

The "I hope to . . ." column captures the group members' dreams, aspirations, plans, and goals for the future. Again, this column may reflect on their loss experience ("I hope my uncle is at peace"); their group experience ("I hope to keep in touch with this group in the future"); and their private, personal goals ("I hope to live a healthy life" or "I hope to graduate high school").

5. Model the activity to the group, using the following guidelines:

As you read your completed Looking Backward . . . Looking Forward worksheet, read the entire "I remember . . ." column before proceeding to the "I am . . ." column, and then read that column in its entirety before ending with the "I hope to . . ." column.

Make sure to repeat the column heading before reading each individual line. For example, "I remember my father tossing me up in the air" or "I remember my first day in this group"; "I am a Capricorn" or "I am sad without my friend."

6. After you answer questions from the group, have the members complete their own Looking Backward . . . Looking Forward worksheets.

Encourage group members to think of several examples for each of the three columns on the worksheet.

The "I am . . ." column may be especially difficult for some adolescents. Some of them may feel compelled to sum up their entire personality, whereas others may limit the type of response they offer by focusing mainly on their physical traits (e.g., "I am tall" or "I have long hair"). You may have to help them by providing additional examples for this column.

You may also have to help group members in other areas, such as brainstorming or simply putting their ideas to paper.

Remind members that they are not required to complete this activity in order, but instead may skip around until they are finished.

If a group member exhibits severe difficulty with or an inability to complete the "I hope . . ." column, this problem may be a warning sign of depression.

As mentioned from time to time in this text, any demonstration of hopelessness or other sign of depression by an adolescent should be assessed further, outside the group setting. If your appraisal leads you to believe that a member is very troubled and possibly suicidal, follow the steps described in the crisis intervention plan in Part I (see chapter 1, "When to Intervene: Characteristic Grieving Patterns and Warning Signs," **pages 18–20).**

7. Once everyone has finished, go ahead and process the activity. A good idea is to have the group members reflect on the activity by asking them the following:

   What was it like to do this activity?

   What feelings did this activity bring up for you?

   Did you find it challenging to think about your entire life path?

   What was more difficult: thinking about the past, the present, or the future? How come?

8. Have group members share aloud their Looking Backward . . . Looking Forward worksheets.

   Just as the Balloon Release activity in Week 9 helped the group members to vent their deep-rooted (and often subliminal) feelings about their loved ones in a unique way and to ease their transition to the ending stage, so does this activity. At this point, adolescents are beginning to accept the realization that the group has an ending.

9. End the session with the closing squeeze.

10. Before leaving the meeting room, make a note to yourself to organize the group members' individual folders that you began creating before the Week 1 session got under way: You will need everything in chronological order for Week 11. Keep in mind that you will also need plenty of time to prepare for this activity, *so allow yourself sufficient time between now and Week 11* to organize the group members' folders and activities.

Looking Backward . . . Looking Forward

Name of group member: _____

Date: _____

I remember . . .	I am . . .	I hope to . . .

Grieving, Sharing, and Healing: A Guide for Facilitating Early Adolescent Bereavement Groups
© 2005 by Rekha Murthy and Lisa-Loraine Smith. Champaign, IL: Research Press (800) 519-2707

Folders and Termination

OBJECTIVE To help group members reminisce about their group experiences, including their achievements and their struggles, and to help make it easier for them to accept the inevitability of the group's termination by exploring their feelings about the group's ending

RATIONALE The process of termination from the adolescent bereavement group parallels the loss experience for group members and may trigger a range of feelings common to the loss of a loved one: Group members identify their feelings, explore their memories, discuss their regrets and hopes, examine the relationships that have developed, and discuss how to maintain any newfound strengths and connections after this type of loss. Termination plays an essential role in a bereavement group in that it highlights the reality of endings and allows for those feelings and thoughts associated with endings to be explored and discussed. What is obvious to group members is that, like life itself, groups also must come to an end.

MATERIALS ▷ Folders containing group members' original work, which were originated by the facilitator prior to the Week 1 session

▷ 1 Feelings Sheet for each member and the facilitator **(p. 164)**

▷ 1 blue and 1 yellow fluorescent marker for each group member

▷ A 6 × 6-inch square of cloth for each member

▷ Dried rosemary for each member

▷ An 8-inch strip of yarn or lace for each member

▷ 1 "Do Not Stand at My Grave and Weep" poem for each member **(p. 165)**

▷ 1 "Celebration of Life Reminder" flyer for each member **(p. 166)**

PROCEDURE

1. Make sure you have each group member's personal folder updated, with everyone's work tucked into the right envelope inside the folder and arranged in the following order from front to back: initial Feelings Sheet, Window to My Soul, original Memorial Poem, typed Memorial Poem, Letter to a Loved One, Looking Backward . . . Looking Forward, and the poem "Do Not Stand at My Grave and Weep."

2. Remind adolescents that there are two weeks remaining in the group and that today the group will be doing activities that will enable them to discuss the group experience and its ending. Have the group recollect that roughly three months ago, when they began, they did an activity that helped them to identify their feelings both about their losses and about joining the group.

   Explain that the group will now repeat this activity, the purpose of which is to identify how they are feeling today—three months later—both about their losses and about their group experience.

3. Pass out the Feelings Sheets and fluorescent markers and have the group use the yellow marker to denote their feelings about having joined the group and the blue marker to denote their feelings about the loss of their loved one.

   Although you modeled this activity in Week 1, you should go ahead right now and participate in the activity at the same time as the adolescents. You, too, have feelings about the group.

   You and the group will process this activity in the next step, when the folders are handed out.

4. Hand out each member's individualized folder, explaining to the group that it contains every piece of work that they have created during their months of participating in the group's activities.

   Ask group members to open their folders at the same time so that everyone is looking through them together.

   Instructing them to begin with the initial Feelings Sheet and continuing in order, from front to back, have the group reflect on their memories of doing each activity and their memories of the group experience as a whole. As the group reminisces, use the following questions as a guide for them as they explore the termination process:

   > Take out your initial Feelings Sheet. At the beginning of the group, what were your thoughts, feelings, and fears about both joining the group and the loss of your loved one?

Compare your initial Feelings Sheet with the one you just completed. How do those feelings you had in Week 1 compare with how you feel now, at the end of the group?

How did all of you relate to each other at the start, and did your relationships change over the course of the group?

Were there particular moments of strength and also moments of struggle?

How did you feel about communication and support within the group?

Did you get what you hoped for from the group?

What do you wish could have been different?

Was there anything you wish there had been more of or less of?

Which activities did you enjoy? Which did you not like?

Were there risks that you took or wish you had taken in exploring your feelings?

How do you feel now that the group is coming to an end?

5. Take this opportunity to discuss with the group the reality of endings, incorporating all of their feelings and thoughts.

As noted earlier, remind them that most things in life have an ending—for example, school, camp, friendships, relationships, and physical existence. Death, therefore, is a part of the life cycle, and the purpose of this group was to make it OK to talk about death and to give support to others and receive support as well.

Although the group is about to come to an end, any strength that was created or connections that were made need not be lost: Encourage the group to maintain their relationships with their peers and to support each other once the group ends, as long as they promise to maintain confidentiality. The latter point is very important: Make sure you remind adolescents that even when the group ends, personal information and stories shared between group members during the group sessions are to remain confidential and should not be shared with those who were not members of the group.

At this point, it is crucial that you keep in mind the importance of preparing adolescents for the group's termination by helping members to express their thoughts, feelings, and regrets about the group experience.

Group members will experience a wide range of feelings (sadness, relief, regret, hope, anxiety) and may regress to behavior more common during group beginnings (acting out, giggling, being disruptive, remaining silent) as the group comes to a close.

As group members face the reality of the group's ending, they know that they will ultimately have to separate from the group. It is up to you to help them identify ways in which they can receive support after the group ends, to help them understand that mutual aid continues long after the group's termination.

If you are concerned about particular group members whom you feel may require continued clinical treatment, be sure to refer them to an appropriate mental health provider who offers individual counseling. This intervention should not be done within the group context, but rather in a one-on-one private conversation with the adolescent and with the knowledge of the parent or guardian.

6. Explain that each group member will be making a Strength Sachet, the purpose of which is to create a permanent symbol and reminder of the group experience. A Strength Sachet is a small pouch made with cloth and filled with dried rosemary, the herb of remembrance.

Instruct group members to choose a square (6 × 6-inch) piece of cloth, place a small handful of dried rosemary in the center, and tie it at the top with an 8-inch strip of yarn or lace.

Tell the group members that they should keep the Strength Sachet as a reminder of the group experience and the strength and struggles they experienced as they moved forward with their lives.

In doing this activity, you are opening up discussion about the inevitability of future losses—and the group will explore their thoughts and fears as well as anything they learned from this group experience that might provide them with support when they face new and different loss situations.

7. Discuss with the group the follow-up or referral information you inserted in their folders, in particular the information that allows them to contact you. In terms of follow-up, be clear about what you and your agency can offer after the group ends, such as reunions or special events. If your agency provides other programs or after-school activities, encourage group members to attend.

8. Have group members take turns reading at least one line each from the poem "Do Not Stand at My Grave and Weep." Invite them to discuss their thoughts about the poem's significance. Be sure to offer your own thoughts, too.

"Do Not Stand at My Grave and Weep" is a healing prayer attributed to the Makah Nation from the northwest coast of Washington State. This poem speaks to the connection we strive to retain when we lose a loved one and explores the permanency of this connection.

9. Inform the group that the next and final week of the group (Week 12) will be the Celebration of Life, in which everyone will bring to the session the favorite food and possibly the favorite music of the loved one. Instruct the group members to do the following:

Take home a copy of the flyer provided at the end of this session. Titled "Celebration of Life Reminder," the flyer will let your parents or guardians know about the event well in advance of Week 12, the last week that the group meets. It will also allow them time to help you prepare food for the celebration or decide to deliver the food to the school the day of the session.

In addition to having members take the flyers home, you may wish to notify parents or guardians by phone to inform them of the event.

Group members may require assistance shopping for or cooking a dish or may need their parent or guardian to drop it off on the day of the event to avoid spoilage. Remind group members that whatever dish they choose to bring, there should be enough for everyone to have some.

10. End the session with the closing squeeze.

Feelings Sheet

Name: _____ Date: _____

Happy	Anxious	Bored	Cautious	Confident	Angry
Committed	Confused	Curious	Don't Care	Frightened	Guilty

Hopeful	Hurt	Interested	Jealous	Lonely
Miserable	Peaceful	Proud	Puzzled	Relieved
Sad	Shocked	Shy	Sorry	Thoughtful

Grieving, Sharing, and Healing: A Guide for Facilitating Early Adolescent Bereavement Groups
© 2005 by Rekha Murthy and Lisa-Loraine Smith. Champaign, IL: Research Press (800) 519-2707

Do Not Stand at My Grave and Weep

Do not stand at my grave and weep

I am not there. I do not sleep.

I am a thousand winds that blow

I am the diamond glints on snow.

I am the sunlight on ripened grain

I am the gentle autumn rain.

When you awaken in the morning's hush,

I am the swift uplifting rush

Of quiet birds in circled flight.

I am the soft stars that shine at night.

Do not stand at my grave and cry.

I am not there: I did not die.

—Anonymous

Celebration of Life Reminder

Dear Bereavement Group Members and Parents and Guardians:

Next week, _____, is our final meeting, and our group will be commemorating our final session—and our 12 weeks together—with a "Celebration of Life," in which we will think back on our group experience and celebrate together with food and music.

Group members: Please bring with you a favorite food of your loved one's—enough for the whole group to enjoy. You may also bring some of your loved one's favorite music.

Parents and Guardians: If your child needs help preparing a dish, please offer your assistance. If you'd like, you're welcome to drop off a dish to the school the day of the celebration. Thank you for your help!

Celebration of Life

OBJECTIVE   For group members to spend their final session in a celebration of the group's success and of life in general, complete with a variety of foods and music that were favorites of everyone's loved one

RATIONALE   The concept of the final day is truly to celebrate—experiences, memories, hopes, and good feelings. In addition to helping members feel connected to one another as well as their loved ones and life in general, the celebration validates the reality that everything ends and that we can feel both sad and happy and still have fun—all at the same time. The celebration sends a healthy message that it is OK to celebrate life and to have fun, even when we are grieving the death of a loved one and are ending a shared experience, such as this group.

MATERIALS   ▷ Favorite foods and CDs and cassettes of loved ones

▷ Eating utensils, beverages, and CD and cassette players (brought by the facilitator)

▷ 1 Group Evaluation Form for every group member (**p. 170**)

PROCEDURE   1. Tell group members that there are few formal instructions for this last session—that the most important thing is that everyone talk, reminisce, laugh, cry, feel, sing, listen to music, dance, dream, share, play, bond, imagine, reflect, and celebrate life!

Keep in mind that the termination discussion during Week 11 is often intense and full of emotion, as group members begin to acknowledge and accept that the group is ending. Although discussion during Week 12 is not absent those same feelings, we have found that an unstructured final session allows group members to be together, to enjoy themselves, and at the same time encourage the expression of a wide range of feelings (e.g., sadness, happiness, anxiety, eagerness). Group members are therefore encouraged to share their feelings (which are then validated) about the group's ending throughout this final session. It should be noted, however, that discussion about the group's termination is not the main focus of Week 12.

2. Encourage each group member to share a little about his or her loved one's favorite food (e.g., what it is, how it is made, when it is eaten). Be sure to ask for information about the loved one's favorite music as well. Most important, let the adolescents enjoy themselves.

   For those group members who may not know what their loved one's favorite dish or favorite music was, let them bring some personal favorites to the celebration.

   Make a point of encouraging everyone to try food they've never tasted before or listen to music they've never heard. By trying different dishes and listening to different music, they will be showing respect for others' uniqueness.

   If at all possible, it is best if the length of this particular session can be extended to an hour and a half; because our bereavement group took place in a school, school officials often allowed the celebration to last for two periods instead of only one.

3. Throughout the session, check in with group members to see how they are feeling about the celebration and what it means to them in light of this being their final group meeting.

4. Sometime during this session, have the group take a few minutes to fill out the short Bereavement Group Evaluation Form on **page 170**. Explain that by filling out the form, they will be helping you to fine-tune the curriculum for the benefit of future adolescent bereavement groups.

5. At some point during the festivities, get the full attention of the adolescents and read to them the following passage, which describes how the celebration and the group's accomplishments look from the vantage point of a veteran bereavement group facilitator. A statement like this is especially fitting for the final week.

Celebrating Our Bereavement Group by Rekha Murthy, CBP facilitator

The Children's Bereavement Project is about creating a safe place where young people can begin to heal a loss that has touched their lives. Old memories are embraced and new ones created as group members talk together, cry, write, draw, and remember. On the last day of our three-month group, we have this "Celebration of Life."

What a feast! *Arroz y frijoles,* chicken with green sauce, *pollo con mole,* cupcakes and tacos! With careful preparation and planning, they brought in the favorite foods of their loved ones who died. They are seven students from different parts of the world who for three months shared their lives with each other—their thoughts, feelings, and emotions about how their lives had changed with the death of a loved one. With food and good company, we celebrated on our last day together—a celebration of life and death, of memories and dreams, of happiness and sadness. In a way, this ending activity was representative of the entire group experience—a mixture of emotions flowing and the realization that it is normal to grieve happily and sadly, to smile and to cry, to regret and to dream. This is what it is all about, the Children's Bereavement Project.

6. End the session with the closing squeeze.

Bereavement Group Evaluation Form

School or Host Agency: _____ **Date:** _____

Please take a few minutes to answer the following questions. Your answers will help us to better understand our strengths and weaknesses so that we can improve the program in which you just participated.

Your answers will remain anonymous: Nobody will know your name or what you wrote. We want your honest opinions. Thank you.

1. Why did you choose to participate in this group? _____

_____

2. Did you get what you hoped for? Why or why not? _____

_____

3. Has the group helped you? If so, in what ways? _____

_____

4. Please tell us about an important or significant moment that you had during the group sessions and why you felt the way you did about it?

_____

_____

5. Was there anything you wish had been different about the group, anything you did not like? If so, what? _____

_____

6. Would you recommend this group to your friends who have experienced a death in their lives? Why or why not? _____

_____

7. Is there anything else you would like to tell us? _____

_____

Afterword

Our years of running the Children's Bereavement Project (CBP) have truly been a journey of strength and inspiration. Looking back, we can see how much greater our understanding is of adolescents in grief. Our skills are improved, our knowledge is increased, and both our insights about death and our understanding of loss have been broadened. Even so, with every group and with every adolescent, we continue to learn something new about death, about life, about our program, and about the needs of a grieving adolescent. We are constantly discovering new ways to hone our program for grieving adolescents. By sharing their thoughts, opinions, and suggestions, these group members are best equipped to help us to evaluate and strengthen our programs. Not to be forgotten, of course, are teachers, parents, and agency personnel, whose feedback is eagerly sought.

EVALUATING THE GROUP EXPERIENCE

It is important to note that evaluating the group experience occurs throughout the entire group, and not only at the end. Accordingly, the purpose and goals of the group are continually evaluated and modified to adjust to members' changing needs (Malekoff, 1997).

Evaluating the group experience can be achieved in both informal and formal ways. Within our groups, which depend on the process of mutual aid, facilitators often check with members to see how they are reacting to the group. Inquiries such as these provide us with the opportunity to assess and reevaluate group members' thoughts regarding the group purpose and other group functions. Furthermore, facilitators rely both on their observations of the group as a whole and of their observations of individual members to assess group outcomes. Communication—both verbal and nonverbal—provides facilitators with important insights as we learn about members' perceptions, reactions, and feelings.

More formal evaluations can be achieved through the creation of surveys or questionnaires that members are then asked to complete. As described in Week 12 of Part II of this book, we have our adolescents fill out an evaluation form on the last day of the group. Because this evaluation allows them to remain anonymous, group members can write freely about their thoughts and experiences during the group as well as their recommendations for the group. We have found these evaluations to be especially helpful in fine-tuning the group structure to meet the particular needs of young people in varied settings.

In addition to receiving feedback on group purpose, we find that it is also important to address any particular problems that may have arisen within the group, along with any specific changes in members' behavior that may have occurred (Malekoff, 1997). Group members themselves are the best sources of evaluative information. During the ending stage of the group, we find that members are both willing and adept at communicating their insights into the group's workings and sharing their thoughts on the group experience. Their personal accounts always serve as priceless tools in evaluating the group experience.

THE VALUE OF FOLLOW-UP

The end of the group may be a difficult time for group members. After three months of working to create a mutual aid environment, members must now come to terms with the fact that the group will no longer exist; rather, after 12 weeks, it will terminate. Yet, even though they must leave the group experience behind, these adolescents may still have both individual and group needs. Grief is not an isolated phenomenon, but one that affects all other areas of a young person's life—schoolwork and extracurricular activities; parental, guardian, and sibling relationships; peer friendships; and so on. Therefore, if possible, it is helpful to link group members to other agency or community services so that they are not left without any supportive outlets. We have found that, although the bereavement group itself cannot be prolonged or re-created, members appreciate the chance to reunite with one another in non-group settings. For example, informal gatherings or reunions may provide adolescents with the opportunity to reconnect with their former group members. Most important, we have discovered that this type of reconnecting can be accomplished without diminishing the impact of terminating from the actual group.

Another method of following up with members is for bereavement group agencies to send out newsletters informing members of any upcoming gatherings or events. The newsletter can also be a forum for members to share their writings about their loss experience, to communicate other thoughts with one another, and to keep members and facilitators up-to-date on their whereabouts as time passes.

Individuals within the group may require further therapeutic assistance after the group ends. Therefore, it is important that facilitators meet with these adolescents and explore various options for continued support, including individual and family counseling and other opportunities. It is especially important for facilitators to help group members who have exhibited signs of depression or suicidal ideation. If this is the case, it is imperative to involve parents and guardians in this process. Without a doubt, when appropriate and necessary, it is essential that facilitators use referrals: It is a critical aspect of follow-up.

Sample Parent/Guardian Permission Slip

(Written on Agency Letterhead)

Date: _____

Dear Parent or Guardian:

Your youngster has expressed interest in joining a group for young adolescents who have lost a family member or close friend to death. I am writing to you because we commonly find that parents and guardians have many questions and concerns about the group. I'll address some of these concerns now, and if you like, talk with you personally. So I invite you to call me. The group will be run by [name of agency], a community-based organization that serves young adolescents.

Both [name of agency] and [name of school] believe that it is important for young people who have lost a loved one to be able to talk with other people who are going through a similar circumstance and can understand much of what they are feeling. The group is not a therapy group; it is a mutual support group—adolescents helping adolescents to cope with a loss. Group members will meet once a week for 12 weeks during the school day [class period and time of class period]. Members are responsible for making up any missed schoolwork, but will receive assistance if needed. The group is facilitated by a [name of agency] professional social worker with years of experience. The information shared in the group is strictly confidential unless it suggests that your child may be facing some type of risk. If a youngster or family requests more individual help, we can arrange that either here or elsewhere.

(Page 1 of 2)

When a young person decides to share personal family business with outsiders, parents or guardians may feel uncomfortable. Many, in fact, worry that a group such as this will be too upsetting for their child and that they in turn will be overwhelmed by their child's sadness. We also understand that some families may cope with death by not talking about it. These are all common and normal reactions.

[Name of agency] has a history of working with adolescents and understands that those who are grieving for a loved one may feel confused, lost, alone, angry, or sad. Young people typically keep their pain to themselves because they don't want to burden their parents or guardians or other family members who also are grieving. This, too, is a normal reaction. But it is very important for children to be able to talk about their feelings in a safe, supportive setting. This group will provide that.

Brochures outlining [name of agency]'s general programming and its school-based bereavement project are enclosed. I hope this letter has helped you to reach a decision about this group. Again, please feel free to call me with any questions you may have. If you decide to give permission for your child to join the group, please fill out the attached permission slip, sign it, and have your child bring it to me at the school by [specified date].

[Name and signature of the contact person from the school]

I, _____, give permission for my child, _____, to attend the 12-week bereavement support group being offered at school. I understand the group will take place during [specified period], from ____ to ____ on _____. If I have any questions concerning my child or the group, I will contact either [name of agency] at [telephone number of agency] or [name of contact person] at [name of school].

[Name and signature of parent or guardian]

_____

_____

(Page 2 of 2)

Grieving, Sharing, and Healing: A Guide for Facilitating Early Adolescent Bereavement Groups
© 2005 by Rekha Murthy and Lisa-Loraine Smith. Champaign, IL: Research Press (800) 519-2707

APPENDIX

B Sample CBP Intake Interview

Name of adolescent: _____ Date of intake: _____

1. Where is your family from originally?

2. What language do you speak at home?

3. When were you born?

4. What grade are you in?

5. Whom do you live with now?

   5a. If you are not living with both parents or guardians, where is your other parent or guardian living now?

6. Have you ever been in a support group before? If so, have you ever been in a bereavement support group?

7. How did you find out about this group?

Note to Interviewer: **Hand page 178 to the adolescents, have them number their top three reasons, and then have them hand the page back to you.**

(Page 1 of 6)

8. Why do you want to be in this group? (From the reasons I am about to give you, please number your top three reasons.)

_____ Want to talk with other students about my feelings

_____ Am feeling sad or depressed

_____ Am finding it hard to concentrate

_____ Feel like harming myself

_____ Feel alone

_____ Worried about how my other family members are dealing with the death

_____ Can't talk with my family

_____ Can't talk with my friends

_____ Think that group members will understand my feelings

_____ Worried that something bad will happen to the people I care about

_____ Want to get out of going to class

_____ Want to do something my friends are doing

_____ Presenter made it sound interesting

_____ Presenter made it sound like something I should do

_____ Other (another reason)

9. Now that I have asked you a few general questions about yourself, I would like to ask you some questions about the loss you have experienced. Who in your life has died? Although only one person may have died, I would like you to tell me if you experienced more than one loss.

Who Died?	When Did They Die?	How Did They Die?

9a. (*Note to intake interviewer:* If there have been multiple losses in the adolescent's life, tell the adolescent the following. If not, go on to No. 10.)

9b. I see that there have been a few people in your life who have died. I am wondering: Can you please tell me whose death in particular has been especially difficult for you? For the rest of the interview, we will discuss only this death. OK? Once we conclude the interview, we can talk about your other losses as well.

10. How did you find out about the death?

11. When did you find out about the death?

12. When you first heard about the death, what was your reaction? (Interviewer should circle response)

Screamed

Cried

Went into shock

Denied that it happened

Felt angry

Acted violently

Felt paralyzed

Other (Please tell me if you had a reaction that I have not mentioned.)

13. Did you know that this person was going to die? For example, was the person sick or terminally ill?

13a. (*Note to intake interviewer:* If the adolescent says yes, ask how long he or she knew that this person was going to die. Then read the following. If the adolescent says no, then ignore the following and go on to No. 14.)

(Page 3 of 6)

13b. Sometimes when people know that someone close to them is going to die, they do certain things to help them prepare for the death. Did you do anything to help you prepare for the death? If yes, what did you do?

14. After a loved one dies, people sometimes do things that help them cope with the loss. I'm going to read a list of things that some people have done to help them deal with their loss. After I read each one, please indicate whether you used this method of coping by answering yes or no. **In the first few months after the death, did you . . .** *(Note to intake interviewer:* When the adolescent answers, circle either yes or no in the appropriate place on the page.)

a. cry often	yes	no
b. pretend the death did not happen	yes	no
c. talk with family members	yes	no
d. talk with friends	yes	no
e. pray	yes	no
f. write down your feelings	yes	no
g. light candles	yes	no
h. talk aloud to your loved one who died	yes	no
i. look at old pictures and possessions	yes	no
j. dream about your loved one who died	yes	no
k. see visions of or your actual loved one around you	yes	no
l. recall times spent with your loved one	yes	no
m. listen to music that reminds you of your loved one	yes	no
n. talk to a photograph of your loved one	yes	no
o. keep busy to avoid thinking about the death	yes	no
p. think happy and pleasant thoughts about the future	yes	no
q. go or ask to be taken to a place of worship	yes	no
r. intentionally harm or abuse yourself physically	yes	no
s. begin or increase harmful behaviors (e.g., smoking, drinking)	yes	no
t. hurt other people physically (e.g., hit, kick, slap)	yes	no
u. say mean things to others	yes	no
v. hit or break objects out of anger or frustration	yes	no
w. other (explain)	yes	no

15. Now I'm going to repeat the list to you and ask you to tell me whether you still use these ways of coping **today.** Do you currently . . .

a. cry often	yes	no
b. pretend the death did not happen	yes	no
c. talk with family members	yes	no
d. talk with friends	yes	no
e. pray	yes	no

(Page 4 of 6)

Grieving, Sharing, and Healing: A Guide for Facilitating Early Adolescent Bereavement Groups
© 2005 by Rekha Murthy and Lisa-Loraine Smith. Champaign, IL: Research Press (800) 519-2707

f. write down your feelings	yes	no
g. light candles	yes	no
h. talk aloud to your loved one who died	yes	no
i. look at old pictures and possessions	yes	no
j. dream about your loved one who died	yes	no
k. see visions of or your actual loved one around you	yes	no
l. recall times spent with your loved one	yes	no
m. listen to music that reminds you of your loved one	yes	no
n. talk to a photograph of your loved one	yes	no
o. keep busy to avoid thinking about the death	yes	no
p. think happy and pleasant thoughts about the future	yes	no
q. go or ask to be taken to a place of worship	yes	no
r. intentionally harm or abuse yourself physically	yes	no
s. begin or increase harmful behaviors (e.g., smoking, drinking)	yes	no
t. hurt other people physically (e.g., hit, kick, slap)	yes	no
u. say mean things to others	yes	no
v. hit or break objects out of anger or frustration	yes	no
w. other (explain)	yes	no

16. Now I would like to ask you how your parent or guardian grieves when a loved one has died. From your observations, how has your parent or guardian reacted to the loss of a loved one?

    a. cried

    b. talked with family members

    c. did not talk with family members

    d. prayed

    e. lit candles

    f. other (explain)

    g. other (explain)

17. Do you feel it is OK to cry in front of your parent or guardian about the death of your loved one?   yes   no

    17a. If not, why not?

18. Do you in fact cry in front of your parent or guardian about the death of your loved one?   yes   no

    18a. If not, why not?

19. There are different people one may feel comfortable talking with after the death of a loved one. When thinking about your loss, do you feel it is OK to talk with the following people? For those whom you choose not to talk with, tell me why.

    a. Mother (or female guardian)   yes no

    b. Father (or male guardian)   yes no

c. Friends or peers	yes	no
d. Family friends	yes	no
e. Teachers	yes	no
f. Guidance counselors	yes	no
g. Siblings	yes	no
h. Other significant people in your life _____	yes	no

20. When thinking about your relationship with your deceased loved one, what regrets do you have (if any), and what do you wish would have been different?

21. Now I'd like to ask you about any cultural or religious traditions your family practices when a loved one dies. If they do, please tell me about them by answering the following questions:

   21a. Was there a ceremony after the death (e.g., funeral, wake)?   yes   no

   If so, what type of ceremony?

   21b. Did you attend the ceremony?   yes   no

   If not, why not?

   21c. Did you help plan the ceremony?   yes   no

   If yes, in what way did you help plan the ceremony?

   21d. Did you participate in the actual ceremony?   yes   no

   If yes, in what way did you participate in the ceremony?

   21e. Do you have any regrets about the ceremony?   yes   no

   If yes, what are your regrets?

22. How important is religion in your family? By religion, I mean, for example, believing in a God or Saints and praying to them.

   22a. Which religion does your **family** practice?

23. Do you consider yourself a religious person?   yes   no

   23a. Which religion do **you** practice?

24. Do you feel that religion has played a part in helping you cope with your loss? If yes, in what way has it helped you?

25. Has the death of your loved one affected your living situation? For example, did you have to change schools because of the death? Are you living with other people as a result of the death?

26. That was the last of my questions. Thank you for your time today. I know I have asked you a lot of questions and that some of them have been difficult to answer. I'm wondering if you have any questions you would like to ask of me. If so, what are they?

(Page 6 of 6)

APPENDIX

C

Sample Group Member Contact Sheet

Sample Group Member Contact Sheet

Name	Address	Phone Number	Parent/Guardian Name(s)	Language spoken at home	Grade/class No.

Grieving, Sharing, and Healing: A Guide for Facilitating Early Adolescent Bereavement Groups
© 2005 by Rekha Murthy and Lisa-Loraine Smith. Champaign, IL: Research Press (800) 519-2707

APPENDIX

D   Service Delivery Steps

1. Send all the information that's necessary (including the letter introducing the agency and the program to the school).
2. Contact the school to verify receipt of information in No. 1 and to discuss program.
3. Set up an appointment with the principal to explain the program in detail.

    In this first meeting, bring the following:

    An information packet describing your agency

    A sample of the Parent/Guardian Permission Slip (Appendix A)

    The Sample Memo to School Personnel (Appendix G)

    The Children's Bereavement Project Overview (Appendix F)

    In this first meeting at the school, do the following:

    Establish a contact person.

    Set up a meeting with school personnel.

    Arrange classroom outreach (when it will be done, who will introduce you, what classes will be targeted).

    Select a time for the bereavement group to meet.

    Secure a confidential area to do intakes as well as a site from which to run the group.

    Establish a plan of action in the event that an adolescent needs to be taken to the emergency room, and decide on the person to contact if such an emergency occurs.

    Pick up a school calendar.

    Ask for a mailbox to use for correspondence.

    Pick up school letterhead stationery to use for the Parent/Guardian Permission Slip.

(Page 1 of 3)

4. On a different day, meet with teachers, guidance counselors, and other key school personnel to explain the project; include procedures and expectations. Hand out the Sample Memo to School Personnel (Appendix G), your agency's brochures, and your business card.

5. Perform classroom outreach in the school, visiting each classroom and using the following outline (For more information on how to conduct classroom outreach, see chapter 3):

How many of you have lost a loved one?

For those of you who have lost a loved one, you are aware that many feelings arise, such as anger, guilt, loneliness, sadness, and a loss of concentration.

We are offering a group in which you can talk about these feelings with other young people who have also suffered a similar loss.

If you are interested in getting more information about joining this group, sign up with the contact person by the end of the day.

The group meets during school hours, so you will need your parent or guardian's permission to attend.

We will meet with you individually and give you a permission slip that you must return to the contact person before the actual intake interview can take place. During this intake interview, together we will determine your appropriateness for joining the group.

Hand out agency brochures that describe the program to those students who are interested.

6. Meet individually with the students who have expressed an interest in joining the group.

Fill out the Group Member Contact Sheet (Appendix C). Information that needs to be filled out includes the students' names, addresses, phone numbers, their parent or guardian's names, the language that is spoken in the home, and the grade/class number.

Ask each potential group member what he or she hopes to get out of participating in the group and to tell you a little about the loved one he or she lost.

Explain the program. Tell each adolescent that sharing thoughts and feelings about the death is expected, as is maintaining confidentiality and completing all schoolwork that will be missed while taking part in the bereavement group.

Explain confidentiality.

Give the Parent/Guardian Permission Slip (Appendix A) to the children and ask them to return it to the contact person by a specified date. This usually means by the end of the week.

Give your agency's brochures and business card to the adolescents.

Call parents or guardians of interested members that night to introduce yourself and the program and to remind them of the permission slip.

7. Check with the contact person in about three days to see how many permission slips have been returned, and encourage him or her to remind the adolescents who haven't yet returned them to do so by the agreed-upon date, which is usually the last day of the week.

8. Conduct intake interviews (Appendix B)

Review the meaning and importance of confidentiality.

9. Fill out the Student Room Schedule (Appendix H).

10. Conduct the bereavement group using the 12-week CBP curriculum.

Bring emergency room information.

Bring a box of facial tissues.

11. During the group, make sure to call the families of the group members to discuss their children's progress and participation in the group. Remember to maintain appropriate confidentiality.

APPENDIX
E

Sample CBP Introduction to Principal Letter

(Written on Agency Letterhead)

Date: _____

Dear [name of school principal]:

As professional social workers employed by Interfaith Neighbors, Inc., we are writing to inform you about a wonderful program for bereaved adolescents that we are offering to junior high and middle school students within your school district.

As you may know, Interfaith Neighbors, Inc., is a nonprofit, nonreligious social service agency committed to providing academic and social/emotional assistance to adolescents. We offer a range of educational, counseling, and skill-building programs for adolescents in the 10- to 15-year-old age range both at our after-school center and at a number of junior high and middle schools. Students who take part in our programs come from many public and parochial schools throughout your catchment area (e.g., Districts 2 and 4). To help you familiarize yourself with some of our services, we have enclosed some brochures describing the programs we offer at our after-school site.

Today, however, we are writing to introduce a specific program: our Children's Bereavement Project (CBP). The CBP offers school-based mutual aid support groups to adolescents who have lost loved ones. We began this program in 1994 after coming to realize that more than 75 percent of the students we worked with had experienced at least one death. We felt it was important for these young people to be able to talk with other adolescents who were in similar situations, and we believed

(Page 1 of 2)

that the school setting was the safest and most comfortable environment in which to offer this unique program. *These groups are not therapy groups; rather, they are support groups in which adolescents learn to help one another cope with their losses.*

The CBP is a 12-week program in which students meet weekly during a designated class period of the school day. The groups are facilitated by a professional social worker with years of clinical experience, and any adolescent who wishes to take part requires permission from a parent or guardian. For the CBP, we have developed a special curriculum that includes a combination of activities and discussion topics that foster group and self-expression: art, writing, reading, poetry, and personal sharing.

We would like to offer this program at your school because we believe that it can benefit everyone. All of our programs at Interfaith Neighbors, Inc., are offered free of charge and on a first-come, first-served basis. We will be contacting you shortly to verify that you received this letter and brochures and to discuss whether you are interested in taking part in the CBP. If you are, we can talk about specific details of the program at that time. If you would like to discuss this program sooner or have any questions, please do not hesitate to contact us at [phone number].

We look forward to working with you and your students.

Sincerely,

[signature]
Rekha Murthy, ACSW

[signature]
Lisa-Loraine Smith, ACSW

Grieving, Sharing, and Healing: A Guide for Facilitating Early Adolescent Bereavement Groups
© 2005 by Rekha Murthy and Lisa-Loraine Smith. Champaign, IL: Research Press (800) 519-2707

APPENDIX

F

Children's Bereavement Project (CBP) Overview

The Children's Bereavement Project (CBP) curriculum takes place during the course of 12 weeks, with group members participating in weekly one-hour sessions. The purpose of our curriculum is to use a combination of activities and discussion topics to create a safe forum in which young people (for the most part, middle and junior high school adolescents 10–15 years of age) can begin to explore the effects of a death on their lives as well as lend support to each other during this process. A variety of different mediums are used to facilitate group and self-expression: art, writing, reading, poetry as well as verbal sharing. Our curriculum has its foundations in social group work theory, meaning that our activities and discussion topics are developed according to what stage the group is in—beginning, middle, or ending (Kurland, 1982; Northen, 1988). The curriculum is structured to facilitate the development of mutual aid, the process by which group members learn to help and support one another (Steinberg, 1997; Malekoff, 1997). The group facilitators also use themselves in purposeful ways by modeling the group's activities. We believe that this kind of sharing of grief experiences facilitates healing as adolescents journey through the grieving process.

BEGINNING STAGE OF GROUP DEVELOPMENT

Activities and discussion topics within the group's beginning stage are designed to help the group members get to know one another and to begin to feel comfortable sharing with each other (Kurland, 1982). To help achieve this objective, the activities within the first four weeks call for less intimate sharing because group members are still becoming comfortable with each other and learning to trust the facilitator, the other members, and the group process itself.

Anticipated Outcomes of the Beginning Stage

To help group members get to know each other, the facilitator, and the group process, including group rules and confidentiality

To create a safe environment in which the facilitator works to build and model trust within the group

To identify and normalize commonalities and differences between the group members with regard to their experiences and feelings

To begin to discuss thoughts regarding death—family patterns of grieving; influence of religion, culture, etc.

To begin to share personal experience of loss

ACTIVITIES

WEEK 1—Feelings Sheet

OBJECTIVE   For group members to introduce themselves and establish commonalities and differences between their feelings about joining the group and their feelings about the deaths of their loved ones

RATIONALE   A Feelings Sheet with a variety of faces expressing different feelings is used to help adolescents identify how they feel about (a) joining the group and about (b) the loss of their loved one. Commonalities and differences are identified and discussed.

WEEK 2—Death Brainstorm Web

OBJECTIVE   Twofold: (a) For group members to use free association as they brainstorm thoughts, feelings, and images connected to the word *death* and (b) to begin the process of introducing their deceased loved ones to the rest of the bereavement group

RATIONALE   Group members brainstorm anything and everything that comes to mind when they see the word **DEATH** written in big, bold letters on a large sheet of paper. This activity allows for the group to work together and to realize the magnitude of thoughts, feelings, hopes, fears, reactions, and experiences that exist among members.

WEEK 3—Guided Reflection through Visualization

OBJECTIVE   To use a creative visualization exercise to help the group deal with their reflections on the death of their loved one, including the following aspects of their experience: how they were told about the death, whether the person or persons who told them about the death were supportive or unsupportive, their role and feelings at the funeral, and any regrets they may have about the loss

RATIONALE   Group members are instructed to sit back, relax, close their eyes, and silently look back in time and recall vividly what happened during their loss experience. By providing a relaxed environment and then asking adolescents a series of questions that gently jog their memories, the facilitator is able to help group members to "see" the events as they occurred at the time of the loss.

WEEK 4—*Without My Dad*

OBJECTIVE   For group members to listen to the facilitator read a short story that was written by a peer—a story that highlights many of the issues involving the loss of a loved one—and then to discuss the themes that affect them personally

RATIONALE   The story, titled "Without My Dad," was written by a 12-year-old named Lucy Yung, a former bereavement group member whose father was murdered by a gunman. This activity enables the grief process by giving members the opportunity to relate to the themes represented in Lucy's story. In other words, whatever issue group members glean from her story will run parallel with what they need to discuss in the group setting. Listening to the story motivates group members to explore their own reactions to the loss of their loved one as well as the coping and adjustment processes that occur both at the time of the loved one's death and after. This story may also serve as inspiration for adolescents to document their own story of loss and to memorialize it forever.

MIDDLE STAGE OF GROUP DEVELOPMENT

The middle stage of the group is composed of activities and discussion requiring more intimate personal sharing, rather than general discussion (Kurland, 1982). By this time, group members have begun to identify what they have in common and what separates their experiences and feelings. Group members begin to communicate with each other and to rely less on the group facilitator for structure. Continued focus is placed on normalizing feelings of grief. From the fifth through the eighth week, increasing emphasis is placed on describing the loved one who died, sharing both positive and negative memories.

Anticipated Outcomes of the Middle Stage

To help group members to communicate and support each other

To allow group members to tell their stories and to explore the pain they feel

To support group members as they remember their loved ones

To help the group to identify the changes and reality of their lives since their loved ones died

To help group members reflect on their feelings of loss, including sadness, anger, depression, and guilt

To allow group members to feel connected to their loved ones, focusing on unresolved feelings

ACTIVITIES

WEEK 5—Window to My Soul

OBJECTIVE   For group members to understand the following truism and to provide their own examples of it: (a) that bereaved individuals often present themselves in a certain way to the outside world, even though they feel differently inside, and that (b) by using the medium of drawing, group members can show the differences between how they feel about their loss and how they portray themselves to others (e.g., family, friends, peers)

RATIONALE   This activity enables the grief process by giving group members the opportunity to explore the many different layers of self that they bring to the grieving process. Having members think about how they present themselves to the outside world and how they truly feel inside serves as a unique exercise that helps them to comprehend the universality of the grieving process. Through discussion, members begin to understand the reasons they present themselves one way to their peers and family members despite feeling a different way inside. By inviting adolescents to reveal their innermost feelings, they feel less isolated and better understood.

WEEK 6—Memorial Poem

OBJECTIVE   To help group members recall and share memories of their loved ones, both positive and negative, commemorating them forever with a Memorial Poem that uses a structured format

RATIONALE   In this activity, group members write a poem in memory of their loved ones, capturing the essence of who these people really were. In a departure from earlier activities, which have focused primarily on the loss experience (i.e., feelings and events having to do with the actual death), the Memorial Poem gives group members an opportunity to recollect the lives and the qualities of their loved ones. By recalling their loved one's qualities—specific likes, dislikes, and hopes—group members begin to see their loved one emerge as a whole person, separate from the adolescent.

WEEK 7—Treasures from the Past

OBJECTIVE To help group members reminisce and discuss memories of their relationship with their loved one by encouraging them to share with the rest of the group the pictures, mementos, and other treasures connected with the loved one that they were asked to bring to the Week 7 session

RATIONALE Week 6 marked the beginning of the discussion of the importance of memories and focused on recollecting the life and qualities of each group member's loved one. Week 7 continues this process by allowing group members to use pictures and objects to fortify their memories of their relationship with the person who died.

WEEK 8—Letters to Loved Ones

OBJECTIVE To help group members compose a letter to their loved one, writing whatever they want to so that it enables them to feel more connected to the person, and then sharing the letter with the rest of the group

RATIONALE Here the adolescent feels connected with the loved one in a unique way. The purpose of the activity is not to have group members offer a permanent goodbye to their loved one; rather, it is about helping group members to say anything and everything they may want to say to their loved one, or to say anything they wished they had said when the loved one was alive.

ENDING STAGE OF GROUP DEVELOPMENT

The ending stage of the bereavement group triggers a range of feelings about loss (Kurland, 1982). Therefore, the last four weeks of the group are structured to allow members to reflect on the group experience and their feelings about having participated. Activities and discussion center on reflecting upon relationships—not only with the deceased, but also with group members and the facilitator. This portion of the group enables members to think about their lives beyond the group, including the potential for future losses.

Anticipated Outcomes of the Ending Stage

To identify unresolved feelings and regrets

To help group members to feel connected to their loved ones

To facilitate group members through the feelings of termination and loss as the group ends

To encourage group members to think about their lives beyond the death they are grieving and toward their life goals

To continue discussion about death, especially about the handling of future losses

To help group members to explore their strengths and struggles, both as individuals and as a group, so that they can recognize what is truly important to them in their lives

ACTIVITIES

WEEK 9—Balloon Release

OBJECTIVE
To help group members symbolically release their thoughts and memories of their loved ones, and at the same time strengthen their connection to their loved ones and to the group as a whole, by releasing helium balloons containing the letters they wrote in Week 8

RATIONALE
Writing their letters in Week 8 offered group members an opportunity to express their thoughts and emotions to and about their loved ones and to maintain a connection with them. By releasing the letters symbolically in Week 9, they fortify this connection by "sending" their letters to their loved ones. In the process, they also begin to take more control over the grieving journey.

WEEK 10—Looking Backward . . . Looking Forward

OBJECTIVE
For group members to write a three-part poem that enables them to look in the past at the people and events that have influenced them, to think about the present and where their life path has taken them thus far, and to look toward the future and what they hope to accomplish

RATIONALE
This session facilitates the grief process by helping group members to view their losses in the larger context of their life paths. Up to this point, group members have focused on their loved ones and their accompanying loss experience. This activity, while still incorporating the loss experience, enables the group to go beyond their losses to explore other facets of their lives.

WEEK 11—Folders and Termination

OBJECTIVE
To help group members reminisce about their group experiences, including their achievements and their struggles, and to help make it easier for them to accept the inevitability of the group's termination by exploring their feelings about the group's ending

RATIONALE
The process of termination from the adolescent bereavement group parallels the loss experience for group members and may trigger a range of feelings common to the loss of a loved one: Group members identify their feelings, explore their memories, discuss their regrets and hopes,

examine the relationships that have developed, and discuss how to maintain any newfound strengths and connections after this type of loss.

WEEK 12—Celebration of Life

OBJECTIVE

For group members to spend their final session in a celebration of the group's success and of life in general, complete with a variety of foods and music that were favorites of everyone's loved one

RATIONALE

The concept of the final day is truly to celebrate—experiences, memories, hopes, and good feelings. In addition to helping members feel connected to one another as well as their loved ones and life in general, the celebration validates the reality that everything ends and that we can feel both sad and happy and still have fun—all at the same time. The celebration sends a healthy message that it is OK to celebrate life and to have fun, even when we are grieving the death of a loved one and are ending a shared experience, such as this group.

APPENDIX

G Sample Memo to School Personnel Based on Interfaith Neighbors' CBP

(Written on Agency Letterhead)

From: Children's Bereavement Project (CBP) of Interfaith Neighbors

Date: _____

Re: Adolescent Bereavement Group Services

Your school has asked Interfaith Neighbors to provide school-based bereavement services to students who are struggling with the loss of a loved one. This memo describes Interfaith Neighbors' **Children's Bereavement Project (CBP)** and details its procedures and timeline as well as your role in the project.

A number of years ago, our Interfaith staff discovered that among the children with whom we work, more than 70 percent had experienced the death of a loved one. We launched the **Children's Bereavement Project** to provide these youngsters with support, understanding, and guidance and to minimize the risk factors associated with childhood and adolescent grief. Studies show that young people who have experienced the loss of a loved one face an increased risk of depression, substance abuse, dropping out of school, involvement with the juvenile justice system, and suicide.

In the **Children's Bereavement Project**, students participate in small groups for 12 continuous weeks during the school day. By providing

(Page 1 of 2)

youngsters with a safe environment with others who *share common experiences,* the process of grief is normalized, and youngsters are helped to feel less isolated and *not so alone.*

The usual procedure for joining a group requires several steps. Students who are interested in the group will be taken out of class on two separate occasions prior to the group's beginning. During the first meeting, students' appropriateness for participating in the group will be assessed. Once a student is deemed appropriate, we will contact his or her parent or guardian for permission and then ask each student to return to us for another period to complete an intake interview about his or her loss. Once this process is completed for all group candidates, the group will begin. If the group takes place during your class period, we will give you a list of participating students. Students are informed that they are responsible for making up any missed class work. However, we ask your help in developing a system to help them with this responsibility.

School personnel have an opportunity to play an important role in this service. Your observations and concerns are very important, and we encourage you to share them with us. This cooperation allows us to develop a more comprehensive support system for the young people in this program. We appreciate your time, understanding, and support in this endeavor. Thank you in advance, and please do not hesitate to call us at [phone number] between [hours available] on [days available] if you have any questions.

[signature]
Rekha Murthy, ACSW

[signature]
Lisa-Loraine Smith, ACSW

H   Sample Student Room Schedule

Sample Student Room Schedule

School: _____   Contact Person/Phone No.: _____

Group Meeting Room: _____   Period: _____ Day: _____

Student	Subject	Teacher	Room/Phone

References

American Psychiatric Association. (1994). *Diagnostic and statistical manual of mental disorders* (4th ed.). Washington, DC: Author.

Attig, T. (1996). *How we grieve: Relearning the world.* New York: Oxford University Press.

Baxter, G., & Stuart, W. (1999). *Death and the adolescent: A resource handbook for bereavement support groups in schools.* Toronto: University of Toronto Press.

Bugental, J. F .T. (1965). *The search for authenticity.* New York: Holt, Rinehart and Winston.

Cho, S., Freeman, E., & Patterson, S. (1979). Adolescents' experience with death: Practice implications. *Social Casework: The Journal of Contemporary Social Work, 63*(2), 88–94.

Fogarty, J. (1998). *The magical thoughts of grieving children: Treating children with complicated mourning and advice for parents.* Amityville, NY: Baywood Publishers.

Fromm-Reichmann, F. (1959). *Psychoanalysis and psychotherapy.* Chicago: University of Chicago Press.

Goldstein, E. (1997). To tell or not to tell: The disclosure of events in the therapist's life to the patient. *Clinical Social Work Journal, 25*(1), 41–59.

Grollman, E. A. (1977). Explaining death to children. *The Journal of School Health, 47*(6), 336–339.

Helping teens cope with death. (1999). Portland, OR: The Dougy Center.

Hodges, M. H. (1988). Adolescent bereavement (Doctoral dissertation, University of Florida, 1988). *Dissertation Abstracts International, 50,* 3138.

Jouard, S. (1971). *Self-disclosure: An experimental analysis of the transparent self.* New York: John Wiley & Sons.

Kandt, V. E. (1994). Adolescent bereavement: Turning a fragile time into acceptance peace. *The School Counselor, 41,* 203–211.

Kubler-Ross, E. (1970). *On death and dying.* New York: Macmillan.

Kurland, R. (1978). Planning—The neglected component of group development. *Social Work with Groups, 1*(2), 173–178.

Kurland, R. (1982). *Group formation: A guide to the development of successful groups.* Albany, NY: Continuing Education Program, School of Social Welfare, State University of New York at Albany and United Neighborhood Centers of America.

Lehmann, L., Jimerson, S., and Gaasch, A. (2001). *Teens together: Grief support group curriculum, Adolescence edition, grades 7–12.* Philadelphia: Brunner/Routledge.

Lloyd, G. (1977). The expression of grief as deviant behavior in American culture. In E. Pritchard et al. (Eds.), *Social Work with the Dying Patient and the Family.* New York: Columbia University Press.

Malekoff, A. (1997). *Group work with adolescents: Principles and practice.* New York: Guilford Press.

Middleman, R., & Wood, G. G. (1990a). *Skills for direct practice in social work.* New York: Columbia University Press.

Middleman, R., & Wood, G. G. (1990b). From social group work to social work with groups. *Social Work with Groups, 13*(3), 3–20.

Northen, H. (1988). *Social work with groups.* New York: Columbia University Press.

Pfeffer, C. R. (1986). *The suicidal child.* New York: Guilford Press.

Rogers, C. (1951). *On becoming a person.* Boston: Houghton Mifflin.

Schoeman, L., & Kreitzman, R. (1997). Death of a parent: Group intervention with bereaved children and their caregivers. *Psychoanalysis and Psychotherapy: The Journal of the Psychoanalytic Institute of the Postgraduate Center for Mental Health, 14*(2), 221–245.

Searles, H. F. (1986). *My work with borderline patients.* New York: Jason Aronson.

Shulman, L. (1992). *The skills of helping individuals, families and groups* (3rd ed.). Itasca, IL: F. E. Peacock Publishers.

Steinberg, D. M. (1997). *The mutual aid approach to working with groups: Helping people help each other.* Northvale, NJ: Jason Aronson.

Sullivan, H. S. (1953). *The interpersonal theory of psychiatry.* New York: W. W. Norton & Company.

Trecker, H. B. (1955). *Social group work: Principles and practices.* New York: Whiteside.

Vickio, C. J. (1999). Together in spirit: Keeping our relationships alive when loved ones die. *Death Studies, 23,* 161–175.

Webb, N. (Ed.). (1993). *Helping bereaved children.* New York: Guilford Press.

Wolfelt, A. (1996). *Healing the bereaved child: Grief gardening, growth through grief and other touchstones for caregivers.* Fort Collins, CO: Companion Press.

About the Authors

Rekha Murthy, MSW, MPH, is a licensed professional social worker and a member of the Academy of Certified Social Workers (ACSW). Her professional career has been dedicated to addressing the arenas of maternal and child/adolescent health from both a mental health and public health perspective. She has provided extensive clinical services, including individual, group, and family therapy, and has presented extensively on various topics pertaining to adolescents, grief, and group work.

As the co-director of the Children's Bereavement Project (CBP) of Interfaith Neighbors, Inc., she helped oversee the expansion and development of this unique program and its featured curriculum. Her clinical observations and empirical research in the area of early adolescents in grief have been featured on both PBS and NPR.

In addition to writing, presenting, and counseling, she has provided supervisory services to master's-level social work students and has taught core social work courses at the university level to undergraduate social work students.

She received both a master of science in social work and a master of public health from Columbia University.

She lives in Chicago with her husband, Mahesh, and their 1-year-old son, Kathan.

Before becoming the executive director of Jewish Family Services of Greenwich in Connecticut, **Lisa-Loraine Smith** was the interim executive director of Interfaith Neighbors, Inc., a nonprofit, community-based social service organization that annually works with more than 500 East Harlem early adolescents and their families. A certified social worker, she was founder and co-director of the Children's Bereavement Project (CBP) since 1994, where she worked comprehensively with early adolescents in grief.

A dynamic speaker, she has presented extensively at conferences and workshops on topics including bereavement, trauma, and stress. After Sept. 11, 2001, she developed the Peace of Mind Project, which was a nationally recognized program offering crisis intervention, support groups, and educational services to more than 900 young people, 500 parents, 2,500 mental health professionals, and 1,200 school personnel.

She has co-authored *Courage After a Crisis: Family and Community Activities for Healing* (2002). She also has been showcased as one of the "Fifteen Amazing Women Who Stole Our Hearts in 2001" in *Working Mother* magazine, February 2002, and been profiled in *Columbia News, the Public Affairs and Record Home Page,* February 2002. She has also been seen on Public Broadcast System (PBS)—*In the Mix,* Dealing with Death (No. 439), 2000—and heard on National Public Radio (NPR)—*The Infinite Mind,* Grief (No. 37), 1998.

In 2002, she graduated from Columbia University, Institute for Not-for-Profit Management, with a certificate in executive leadership. In 1990, she received a certificate in group psychotherapy from the Eastern Group Psychotherapy Society in New York City, and in 1988 she graduated from Yeshiva University, Wurzweiler School of Social Work.

She is living in New Jersey and is happily married to her loving husband, Jerry Gips. They have a 6-year-old daughter, Anya Esther Smith Gips.